THE POWER OF PHENOMENOLOGY

The Power of Phenomenology took form when the two authors realized that a single theme has run through the course of their almost half-century-long collaboration like a red thread—namely, the power of phenomenological inquiry and understanding in a wide range of contexts.

This book demonstrates how they have experienced the power of phenomenology in their therapeutic work with patients, especially those struggling with horrific trauma; in their encounters with psychological and philosophical theories; and in their efforts to comprehend destructive ideologies and the collective traumas that give rise to them. *The Power of Phenomenology* presents the trajectory of this work. Each chapter begins with a contribution written by one or both authors, extending the power of phenomenological inquiry to one or more of these diverse contexts. The contributions are followed, one or two at a time, by a dialogue between the authors, illustrating the dialectical process of their long collaboration. The unusual format seeks to bring the phenomenology of their collaborative efforts to life for the reader.

The Power of Phenomenology will appeal to psychoanalysts, psychoanalytic psychotherapists, and scholars of philosophy.

Robert D. Stolorow is a Founding Member at the Institute of Contemporary Psychoanalysis, Los Angeles, USA. He is the author of *World, Affectivity, Trauma: Heidegger and Post-Cartesian Psychoanalysis* (Routledge, 2011) and *Trauma and Human Existence: Autobiographical, Psychoanalytic, and Philosophical Reflections* (Routledge, 2007) and co-author of eight other books.

George E. Atwood is Emeritus Professor of Psychology at Rutgers University and a Founding Member of The Institute for the Psychoanalytic Study of Subjectivity, New York, USA. He is the author of *The Abyss of Madness* (Routledge, 2011) and co-author of seven other books with Robert D. Stolorow. Both he and Stolorow have been absorbed for nearly five decades in the project of rethinking psychoanalysis as a form of phenomenological inquiry.

THE POWER OF PHENOMENOLOGY

Psychoanalytic and Philosophical Perspectives

Robert D. Stolorow and George E. Atwood

LONDON AND NEW YORK

First published 2019
by Routledge
2 Park Square, Milton Park, Abingdon, Oxon OX14 4RN

and by Routledge
711 Third Avenue, New York, NY 10017

Routledge is an imprint of the Taylor & Francis Group, an informa business

British Library Cataloguing in Publication Data
A catalogue record for this book is available from the British Library

Library of Congress Cataloging in Publication Data
Names: Stolorow, Robert D., author. | Atwood, George E., author.
Title: The power of phenomenology : psychoanalytic and philosophical perspectives / Robert D. Stolorow and George E. Atwood.
Description: New York : Routledge, 2019. | Includes bibliographical references and index.
Identifiers: LCCN 2018026212 (print) | LCCN 2018033654 (ebook) | ISBN 9780429448584 (Master) | ISBN 9780429828140 (Web PDF) | ISBN 9780429828133 (ePub) | ISBN 9780429828126 (Mobipocket/Kindle) | ISBN 9781138328525 (hardback : alk. paper) | ISBN 9781138328563 (pbk. : alk. paper) | ISBN 9780429448584 (ebk)
Subjects: LCSH: Phenomenology.
Classification: LCC B829.5 (ebook) | LCC B829.5 .S67265 2019 (print) | DDC 142/.7—dc23
LC record available at https://lccn.loc.gov/2018026212

ISBN: 978-1-138-32852-5 (hbk)
ISBN: 978-1-138-32856-3 (pbk)
ISBN: 978-0-429-44858-4 (ebk)

Typeset in Bembo and Stone Sans
by Florence Production Ltd, Stoodleigh, Devon, UK

To the memory of Emily S. Stolorow

CONTENTS

Preface *ix*

1 The phenomenological circle and the unity of life and thought 1

2 Seeds of psychoanalytic phenomenology: A formative clinical experience 21

3 Credo—Phenomenological explorations and reflections 37

4 Credo—Intersubjective-systems theory: A phenomenological-contextualist perspective 57

5 Emotional disturbance, trauma, and authenticity: A phenomenological-contextualist perspective 71

6 The phenomenology of language and the metaphysicalizing of the real 85

7 Experiencing selfhood is not "a self" 91

8 Phenomenology and metaphysical realism 97

9 Phenomenological contextualism and the finitude of knowing 105

10 Walking the tightrope of emotional dwelling 113

11 There must be blood: The price of emotional dwelling 119

12 Concluding dialogue 127

References *131*
Index *137*

PREFACE

The idea for this book took form when we realized that a single theme has run through the course of our nearly half-century-long collaboration like a red thread—namely, the power of phenomenological inquiry and understanding in a wide range of contexts. We have experienced the power of phenomenology in our therapeutic work with patients, especially those struggling with horrific trauma; in our encounters with psychological and philosophical theories; and in our efforts to comprehend destructive ideologies and the collective traumas that give rise to them. This book presents the trajectory of this work.

Each chapter begins with a contribution written by one or both of us, extending the power of phenomenological inquiry to one or more of these diverse contexts. These contributions are followed, one or two at a time, by a dialogue between us, illustrating the dialectical process of our long collaboration. Our hope is that this unusual format will help bring the phenomenology of our collaborative efforts to life for the reader.

Ten of the 12 essays were taken from previously published work. Chapter 1 was originally published in *The Psychoanalytic Review* (2016, 103, 291–316). Chapters 3, 4, and 10 were published in *Psychoanalytic Dialogues* (2013, 23, 383–389; 2015, 25, 137–152; 2016, 26, 102–107) and are reprinted by permission of Taylor & Francis, LLC. Chapter 5 first featured in *Existential Medicine* (ed. K. Aho, 2018, Rowman and Littlefield International, 17–25). Chapter 6 first appeared in *Language and Psychoanalysis* (2017, 6, 4–9). Chapter 7 first featured in *International Journal of Psychoanalytic Self Psychology* (2016, 11, 183–187) and is reprinted by permission of Taylor & Francis, LLC. Chapter 8 featured in *Existential Analysis* (2018, 29, 45–48), and Chapter 9 in *The Humanistic Psychologist* (2018, 46, 204–210). Chapter 11 first appeared in *The American Journal of Psychoanalysis* (2017, 77, 399–405) and is reprinted by permission of Palgrave MacMillan. We thank the editors and publishers of these articles and chapters for their permission to reuse this work.

We are deeply grateful to Liz Atwood and Julia Schwartz for their unfailing support and encouragement during some very difficult times for all of us.

1

THE PHENOMENOLOGICAL CIRCLE AND THE UNITY OF LIFE AND THOUGHT[1]

> It has gradually become clear to me what every great philosophy has heretofore been: a confession on the part of its author and a kind of involuntary and unconscious memoir.
>
> (Friedrich Nietzsche, 1886, section 6, p. 203)

In what follows, we tell the story of two love affairs with philosophy—first, George Atwood's, and second, Robert Stolorow's. We also describe the interaction of our respective philosophical journeys in our collaborative studies over the last four decades. Our goal in giving this account is to reflect on the deepest assumptions of the phenomenological-contextualist theory to which our shared efforts have led us. Again and again, we have been led to the inseparability of theoretical thought and the life in which it emerges.

1. George Atwood

I found philosophy at the age of 16 when I ran across a little book on *pragmatism*, a work that summarized aspects of the thinking of William James, Charles Sanders Pierce, and John Dewey. I cannot say that I found the ideas in this book terribly exciting in themselves, but I was able to understand them well enough, and there was something about the nature of the thinking described that was utterly entrancing to my young mind. I had discovered philosophy, a field of thought that seemed to be devoted to searching for the ultimate meaning of life and for the universal principles according to which one can and should live. It had not previously occurred to me that such an interesting realm of study even existed.

This first impression became more complex a year later as I began my undergraduate education at the University of Arizona and enrolled in a course on the history of philosophy. I saw to my astonishment that there were whole territories of questions with which philosophers occupied themselves, interesting questions about the nature of reality, the process of knowing, good and evil, mind and body, about the nature of the beautiful, of meaning, of freedom, of truth, and of being itself. The pull was very strong to embrace this incredible discipline, but I was also drawn in a different direction in these early years of my academic studies—toward psychiatry as a career. Concurrently with encountering philosophy, I also discovered psychoanalysis, in the works of Freud and Jung, and was so taken with their discoveries and theories that I decided to follow in their footsteps. This meant undergoing medical training, as they had, then a residency in psychiatry, and eventually becoming a psychotherapist and, I hoped, a theorist of human nature. What career, I asked, could possibly be as good or as interesting? I could dwell for a lifetime in the study of dreams and their symbolism, investigating madness in its many forms and variations, researching the mysteries of human psychological development. Psychoanalysis appeared to me to be a window into the human soul, one that had just begun to be opened by the great theorists of the field. There was a vast country coming into view, and I was to become one of its explorers, a discoverer of continents unknown. And, in such exploration, it seemed possible that one might run across the foundational constituents of human nature.

The premedical program at my college was very demanding, and after a few courses I ran into a wall—organic chemistry. Picture the following scene: an intensely unhappy 18-year-old George Atwood, in his second semester of this course, clad in a smock and wearing protective goggles, holes in his trousers from an earlier acid spill, utterly exhausted and heavily perspiring, holding up a test tube filled with a foul-smelling black goo. This was the product of 12 consecutive hours of effort to synthesize an organic compound in a process that should have only required perhaps two hours. I have forgotten what the target compound was, but it was supposed to appear as a beautiful, light purple powder. And what had I created? Black, stinking goo. It was not the first time my laboratory exercises had ended in such a mess. Words came into my consciousness: *I just ain't cut out for this.* Looking ahead to other difficult courses—in biochemistry, physiology, anatomy, and then medical school to be followed by an internship—I shuddered at the thought of the many years of toil that would have to be survived, studying things at a great remove from what had inspired me. So, I opted for psychology as a major area of study instead. I imagined psychoanalysis to be a central part of the discipline of psychology, and additionally it seemed to me that psychology overlapped substantially with my beloved philosophy.

Following the path of my subsequent education, undergraduate and graduate, presented new difficulties. The programs at the University of Arizona and subsequently at the University of Oregon were unsympathetic to psychoanalysis and very distant from philosophy, promoting instead behaviorist theories and methods, and insisting on quantitative empirical research. I continued my psychoanalytic education on a separate basis nevertheless, by purchasing and reading the complete works of Freud and Jung, and by collecting and studying major writings of other psychoanalytic theorists as well. Gazing back in time, I see how hard I was trying somehow to fit my psychoanalytic and philosophical interests into the prevailing paradigm of empirical research. My first publication, still as an undergraduate, was a quantitative experiment dealing with the existential philosophical theme of mortality anxiety—"Anxiety and two forms of cognitive resistance to the idea of death" (Golding, Atwood, and Goodman, 1965).

The explorations in philosophy proper also continued. One of my last undergraduate courses, taken in 1965, was in existentialism, and the readings for this course included selections from the book *Existence* (May, Angel, and Ellenberger, 1958). The essays by Rollo May and even more one by Ludwig Binswanger led me then to Martin Heidegger's (1927) *Being and Time*. I found Heidegger's masterwork exceptionally difficult to understand but endlessly fascinating, and I kept a copy of his book at my bedside, for years reading short passages from it almost every night. When I was unable to sleep, I would open it to any random page and peruse the long, often incomprehensible sentences. I also read widely in other philosophers, some of my favorites being Immanuel Kant, Søren Kierkegaard, Friedrich Nietzsche, Edmund Husserl, and Jean-Paul Sartre. I recall standing for long hours in the stacks of the University of Oregon library reading Maurice Merleau-Ponty's (1945) *Phenomenology of Perception*, another book that was intriguing but extremely dense and difficult to follow.

Something happened to my mind in consequence of these philosophical readings, especially those in phenomenology. Looking back, it seems to me that this early exposure awakened me from my Cartesian trance. Formerly, without any explicit awareness, I had believed in the existence of the mind, in there being an inner mental life that somehow was separate from a surrounding outer world. I thought that people had minds, and that I possessed one too. I remember arguments, some of them heated, with fellow students as I began to question the existence of an "inner world" that exists separately from "external reality." One of these, a woman with whom I had become personally involved, told me that to question the existence of the mind—of an inner mental life that stands apart from the outer world—is like denying that the sun rises in the morning. The thought came to me that her personal reality was split between external and internal, perhaps somehow by trauma, and that she was universalizing her own psychological division by assuming its presence as a given in everyone's life. Our discussions broke down at this point, as did our personal relationship not long thereafter. In the meantime, I had begun to think that there is no such thing as the mind; there is just experience, just consciousness, just the subjective, which is neither internal nor external.

I continued to adapt to my academic program, conducting experiments as required, and finally completed a doctoral degree. What followed was a post-doctoral fellowship in clinical psychology at the Western Missouri Mental Health Center in Kansas City, under the guiding supervision of Austin Des Lauriers, the author of *The Experience of Reality in Childhood Schizophrenia* (1962). Des Lauriers was my first great mentor figure, and he was a phenomenologist. His theory of the central disturbance constituting so-called schizophrenia was that it involves a loss of reality experience—i.e., a loss of the sense that anything is real, substantial, and enduring—and a consequent devastation of the experience of selfhood as it loses its boundaries, cohesion, and continuity in time.

My postdoctoral years, occupied primarily with working on an inpatient service for very severe psychiatric disorders, were decisive in shaping my destiny as a clinician and as a theorist. I gave myself unreservedly to the work, spending up to 70 hours a week at the hospital, getting to know a great many of the patients not formally assigned to me and taking voluminous notes on all my experiences. Under my mentor's influence, I tried to focus on understanding the patients I met phenomenologically, in terms of what their experiences were as best I could make them out. Some of these experiences I had never encountered before, and, when I tried to find sense in what was being said to me in terms of the many theories I had studied, I got nowhere. I recall hearing from a number of people, for example, that the world had come to an end and that they were dead rather than alive. How, I wondered, would Freud, or Jung, or Sullivan, or any of a whole range of other theorists interpret such expressions? The regular psychiatric staff members at the hospital viewed these statements as delusional, as symptoms of an underlying psychosis that was causing the patients to lose contact with the objectively real. This way of thinking seemed utterly, woefully inadequate. I met other patients who made the claim to be God, to be the savior of the universe, and still others who told me that *I* was God and had the power to set all things in the world straight and right. I had an event occur on the very first day of my postdoctoral work that set me reeling: as I walked out of the elevator and on to the floor where the patients were housed, a very tall and heavy bipolar patient threw herself upon me and attempted to engage in sexual intercourse. One of the first to tell me she was dead, as we sat in an office for our interview, lit a cigarette I gave her and pressed its burning tip into the flesh on her arm as she looked into my eyes and smiled warmly. I also remember a young man I met in this very early period who was silent for long periods, not responding to my queries and not looking at me as I tried to engage him–finally he spoke, saying that he was hearing a voice saying "Kill Dr. Atwood." A woman, 60 years old, was brought to the hospital by the Secret Service after attempting to break into the home of ex-President Harry Truman, then still alive and residing nearby. She said that she had traveled to his home to retrieve her head, which had been stolen from her and placed under his control as part of a terrible conspiracy. A young woman I eventually worked closely with for many years introduced herself to me one evening with the claim that she had just experienced sexual intercourse with Jesus Christ. It was like that—case after case, one incomprehensible story after another, one strange pattern of behavior followed by another one, and all with no explanations and nothing in my background to help me begin to know what it was I was seeing. Although I had earned a Ph.D. in clinical psychology, I saw that I knew nothing and had to forget all I had learned in my so-called education and start over again, from scratch. I recognized that the nurses and the aides and even the cleaning staff at the hospital, those who pushed the brooms and took care of the laundry, were way ahead of me. They had seen and known these patients for years, and were on familiar terms with things that I was encountering for the very first time in my life.

My appreciation of phenomenology increased dramatically because of these and other such continuing challenging experiences. Phenomenology itself is always trying to start over again, to find the requisite starting point from which to approach the task of describing and understanding subjectivity. With sustaining support from Austin Des Lauriers, it became possible to embrace the task of my own new beginning, with the goal of discovering the meanings of the many forms of madness by which I was confronted. How did I know there were meanings there to be found? In accord with the entire enterprise of psychoanalytic theory, I made the assumption that this was so, and went on from there.

From my point of view now, gazing back in time, I think I understand an important part of my difficulty in applying the psychoanalytic concepts I had studied. I did not know it at the time, but it was because of a profound disjunction between the philosophical assumptions underlying the theoretical systems I was trying to use, and the nature of the extreme psychological disturbances with which I was beginning to engage. Here is how I put it in a paper, co-authored by my colleagues Robert Stolorow and Donna Orange, some 30 years later:

> [T]he experiences that characterize these psychological disturbances tend to cluster around themes of personal annihilation and the destruction of the world. Such experiences occur outside the horizons of Cartesian systems of thought, which rest upon a vision of the mind as an isolated existent that stands in relation to a stable, external reality. The Cartesian image of mind, rigidly separating an internal mental subject from an externally real object, reifies and universalizes a very specific pattern of experience, centering around an enduringly stable sense of personal selfhood that is felt as distinct and separate from a world outside. Experiences of extreme self-loss and the disintegration of the world cannot be conceptualized within such an ontology of mind, because they dissolve the very structures this ontology posits as universally constitutive of personal existence.
>
> (Atwood, Orange, and Stolorow, 2002, p. 144)

In the early years I am describing, I was unable to articulate any of this and certainly could not theoretically conceptualize my patients' psychological situations; but I found it possible nevertheless to relate to them on a practical level and discuss with them all they were undergoing. When people told me that they were dead because someone had drained their bodies of all their blood, I heard what had been said not as delusion but just as experience, one of infinite devitalization. Similarly, if I was told that I possessed godlike powers, I believed this was what was being felt—George Atwood, creating (and perhaps destroying) personal universes. When someone explained to me that his wife and child had been replaced by persecuting duplicates, I did not pronounce his thoughts to be insane.

Instead, I just listened to him, and wondered about the overall calamity that had befallen him, when his most intimate family members could no longer be relied upon even to be themselves. If I met a person whose body was covered with scars from years and even decades of self-cutting, I did not diagnose the presence of so-called borderline personality disorder. Instead, I tried to decipher the messages to the world that the scars from the cuts were trying to send forth. In other words, I was searching for a human understanding of each and every patient I met, and simultaneously for a set of guiding ideas to draw upon to support that search.

There was one indelible impression I took away from my postdoctoral years. It concerned the healing power of psychotherapy in the most severe psychological disturbances. Working intensively with a number of patients, guided by indispensable consultations with Des Lauriers, I saw with my own eyes dramatic recoveries from chronic mental illnesses arising out of a human intervention. Such experiences laid the foundation for a deep optimism that I have brought to all my subsequent clinical work.

2. Robert Stolorow

I first touched on the edges of philosophy at the age of 13 when I read a book on the life and work of Albert Einstein, which eventually became the topic of my high school senior thesis. Foreshadowing my later career as a subversive thinker, I scandalized the congregation with my Bar Mitzvah sermon on Einstein's conception of God as an impersonal principle of order in the universe.

Influenced by my father's admiration of philosophy, as an undergraduate at Harvard I eagerly took courses in Plato's *Republic*, Aristotle's *Ethics*, Augustine's *Confessions*, aesthetics, and intellectual history. A nodal point occurred when, in Gordon Allport's course on personality psychology, I encountered Rollo May's book, *Existence*. Like George, I became fascinated with the thought of Martin Heidegger and Ludwig Binswanger.

Despite my passion for philosophy, I formed an interest in doing hard-science research in psychopathology and decided that the best path toward that ambition was medical school and psychiatry. I enrolled at Cornell Medical School in the fall of 1964, but I was a very unhappy camper there and dropped out after five weeks, deciding that the most appropriate path for my goal was doctoral studies in clinical psychology, which I pursued back at Harvard the next year. Paralleling George's disaster in organic chemistry lab, my own performance in anatomy lab was so atrocious that I think it is safe to say that many lives have been saved as a result of taking a scalpel out of my hands. The year before beginning graduate work at Harvard proved pivotal, as I enrolled in a course at the New School on existential psychology given by Rollo May. I was entranced by May's lectures on phenomenology and existential philosophy—the works of Husserl, Heidegger, and Sartre. I also read May's (1950) book, *The Meaning of Anxiety*, which introduced me to the concept of *ontological anxiety*, a concept that was to become very important to me in later years. The following year, in a seminar given by Robert

White, I wrote a term paper exploring the anxiety-defense process from three perspectives—the intrapsychic, the interpersonal, and the ontological—which became my first published article (Stolorow, 1969).

As a doctoral student in clinical psychology, I soon became disillusioned with empirical psychological research, feeling that it stripped psychology of everything humanly meaningful. I contacted a former undergraduate professor, Henry Aiken, then at Brandeis University, and proposed doing a second doctorate in philosophy, with an eye toward using phenomenology and existential philosophy to clean up the mess of psychoanalytic theory. Aiken was enthusiastic about my proposal, but, during my subsequent clinical internship, I found that I really enjoyed psychoanalytic work and, after completing my doctorate in psychology, I decided to go to New York to pursue psychoanalytic training instead. My idea of pursuing doctoral studies in philosophy had to await several decades before coming to fruition.

Like George, I early on became interested in the phenomenological underpinnings of clinical phenomena. Drawing on David Shapiro's (1965) concept of neurotic styles, my doctoral dissertation examined the differing causality interpretations characteristic of obsessive versus hysterical styles, with the former showing an exaggerated sense and the latter an attenuated sense of personal causation. In my first year of psychoanalytic training, I published a brief article, "Mythic Consonance and Dissonance in the Vicissitudes of Transference" (Stolorow, 1970), exploring the impact on the therapeutic relationship of correspondences and discrepancies between the causality interpretations of patient and therapist. This early article anticipated our later conception of the therapeutic relationship as an intersubjective system. Two years later, I published another brief article whose title explicitly named *phenomenology*—"On the phenomenology of anger and hate" (Stolorow, 1972), exploring how the experience of these emotions differs depending on whether forgiveness is felt to be a possibility.

Early in my psychoanalytic training, I also became interested in Heinz Kohut's (1966, 1968) work on narcissism and the treatment of narcissistic disorders. It seemed to me that hidden within Kohut's obscure drive-theoretical language—the language of the Freudian orthodoxy against which I was already in vigorous rebellion—were important insights into the relationships that either fostered or undermined the senses of self-cohesion, self-continuity, and self-esteem. What was crystallizing for me here was a focus on emotional phenomenology and its intersubjective contexts, which would soon become the joint preoccupation of our collaborative work. Foreshadowing my later preoccupation with emotional trauma and efforts to rethink the concept of the unconscious, my first psychoanalytic control case was a very successful treatment of a woman whose sense of self had been massively damaged by her ways of denying an early devastating traumatic loss.

* * *

By the time George and I met at Rutgers in 1972 and began our long collaborative dialogue, we had arrived at similar positions of profound dissatisfaction with the prevailing frameworks of our field and their official languages—those of traditional diagnostic psychiatry in the case of George and that of Freudian metapsychology in that of my own. In each instance, the prevailing framework and language seemed to alienate us from the very experiences we wished to engage and understand. We each sensed the need for a framework that was always and only about emotional experience and how it came to be shaped. We were ripe for a collaborative effort at creating a psychoanalytic phenomenology.

3. George Atwood

Robert Stolorow and I met in the spring of 1972, when he was offered a faculty position at Rutgers University. At the time, an effort was being made to assemble a group of scholars at Rutgers, under the leadership of Silvan Tomkins, to resurrect the personological tradition in psychology that originally had been associated with Henry Murray at Harvard University. This tradition is defined by its central methodology—the intensive, in-depth case study, providing an alternative to the emphasis of academic psychology on quantification and objective empirical research. I called Bob and urged him to accept the offer that had been made, telling him he would be insane to go anywhere else. I told him that in our working together there was the possibility of significant advances in the sort of personality theory to which both of us were already deeply committed. He accepted the offer and our collaboration began.

There were many wonderful lunchtime conversations over cheeseburgers and endless cups of coffee in the first and second years of our relationship. We discussed anything and everything about personality psychology—its past, present, and future. In one of these early talks, as I recall it—now more than four decades later—a question was posed: "What is the most important problem facing the field of personality theory today?" One of us—I no longer remember which one—offered a succinct answer: "That would be the problem of understanding the dimensionalization of a person's experiential world." The use of the term *world* reflected already our shared background and interest in existential phenomenology and foreshadowed much that was to come in the many years of our work that followed. The word *dimensionalization* in this phrasing, influenced to some degree by the thinking of Silvan Tomkins, was intended to capture the idea that every person's world has its own unique emotional geometry, rendered visible in repeating, invariant patterns of experience and conduct.

In another of these initial conversations, an idea was floated bearing similarity to the one just described. We were talking about Bob's psychoanalytic training in New York City at the Postgraduate Center for Mental Health, then in its final stages. The role of the so-called structural model in that training came up in our discussion, the tripartite division of the mind into ego, id, and superego. I remember Bob describing how this conceptualization had been taught as if "this is just the way human beings come packaged"—in other words, as a universally valid description of the mind. I responded: "Perhaps, though, the tripartite model is not universal but is just a symbol, one that points to an important but still particular class of conflictual experiential states." Implicit here was an incompletely developed intuition that some personal worlds of emotional experience might be organized or structured along the Freudian lines, but that very different models of the mind might apply to other such worlds. We were beginning to imagine the existence of a wide range of variations and were also starting to see that different schools of thought in psychoanalytic personality theory somehow corresponded to these differing variations. What was not apparent, however, was how to move toward a more comprehensive psychoanalytic phenomenology, a more general framework addressing personal worlds in all their diversity, richness, and idiosyncrasy.

Soon thereafter, however, an approach to this problem opened up to us, in our collaborative studies of the subjectivity of personality theory. We saw that each of the classic schools of psychoanalytic thought had its own central affective theme, and that this theme was also the organizing emotional dimension of the theorist's personal world. An analysis of the personal subjectivity of these various frameworks, we began to recognize, opened a pathway to a more general point of view—in Bob's words, "a movement from studies of the subjectivity of theory to a theory of subjectivity itself." Our first book, *Faces in a Cloud: Subjectivity in Personality Theory* (Stolorow and Atwood, 1979) was an effort to follow this pathway and reach toward an embracing psychoanalytic phenomenology.

4. Robert Stolorow

In these early years of our collaboration, the philosophy that attracted my interest largely took the form of George S. Klein's brilliant work on the nature of psychoanalytic theory. Klein (1976) claimed that Freud's psychoanalytic theory actually amalgamates two theories—a metapsychology and a clinical theory—deriving from two different universes of discourse. Metapsychology (which we eventually recognized as a form of metaphysics) deals with the material substrate of experience and is couched in the natural science framework of impersonal structures, forces, and energies. Clinical theory, by contrast, deals with intentionality and the unconscious meanings of personal experience, seen from the perspective of the individual's unique life history. Clinical psychoanalysis asks "why" questions and seeks answers in terms of personal reasons, purposes, and individual meanings. Metapsychology asks "how" questions and seeks answers in terms of the nonexperiential realm of impersonal mechanisms and causes. Klein sought to disentangle metapsychological and clinical concepts, retaining only the latter as the legitimate content of psychoanalytic theory. For Klein, the essential psychoanalytic enterprise involves the reading of disclaimed intentionality and the unlocking of unconscious meanings from a person's experience, a task for which the concepts of the clinical theory, purged of metapsychological contaminants, are uniquely suited.

Although Klein did not chronicle the philosophical traditions that informed his proposal for a radical "theorectomy" for psychoanalysis, he had unveiled its clinical essence as a hermeneutic phenomenology devoted to the investigation of the meanings that unconsciously shape experiential life. I was so taken with his proposal that I agreed to review an anthology of articles about it for *Contemporary Psychology* (Stolorow, 1976). Much more important for the evolution of our own theoretical framework, I wrote an article, "The concept of psychic structure: Its metapsychological and clinical psychoanalytic meanings" (Stolorow, 1978), applying Klein's distinction to the psychoanalytic concept of psychological structure. I suggested that, in contrast to metapsychological structures like id, ego, and superego, in its clinical psychoanalytic meanings *psychological structure* denotes the principles that prereflectively organize an experiential world. With this conception of psychological structure, psychoanalysis became a form of inquiry explicitly rooted in the tradition of Continental phenomenology, investigating prereflective structures of experience.

5. George Atwood and Robert Stolorow

Our second book, *Structures of Subjectivity: Explorations in Psychoanalytic Phenomenology* (Atwood and Stolorow, 1984), included three developments in our ever-evolving interaction with philosophy. First, we offered a more detailed explication of our own philosophical premises in fashioning a phenomenological reconceptualization of psychoanalytic theory:

> The point of departure of psychoanalytic phenomenology is the concept of [the person as] an experiencing subject. This means that at the deepest level of our theoretical constructions we are operating within a sphere of subjectivity, abjuring assumptions that reduce experience to a material substrate. The material world, from our standpoint, is regarded as a domain of experience, and the concepts of natural science are understood as modes of organizing that domain of experience. This is in contrast to a theoretical [and philosophical] position that would assign ontological priority to physical matter and interpret human consciousness as a secondary expression of material events. The development of knowledge in the sciences of nature involves the organizing and interconnecting of human observations, which are experiences; but materialism is a doctrine based on *reifying* the concepts of natural science and then seeing consciousness as an epiphenomenon of those reifications.
>
> (Atwood and Stolorow, 1984, p. 7)

The second development in our relationship with philosophy occurring at the time appeared in a systematic comparison of our emerging ideas with those of three great phenomenologists—Edmund Husserl, Martin Heidegger, and Jean-Paul Sartre. Although we were still picturing psychoanalytic investigation as distinct from philosophical inquiry, we sought to define the essential similarities and differences of philosophical and psychoanalytic phenomenology:

> Each of the 3 phenomenological systems reviewed . . . is a proposal concerning the assumptions underlying the study of human experience. These proposals have in common an emphasis on differentiating between the properties of material objects in the world of experience and the properties of subjectivity itself. This same emphasis has been of growing importance in recent psychoanalytic thought, specifically in the critique of Freudian metapsychology. It seems to us that this agreement establishes the possibility of an integration of phenomenological insight into psychoanalysis.
>
> (Atwood and Stolorow, 1984, p. 30)

We noted two obstacles to such integration—the commitment of analysts to a vision of their field modeled on the sciences of material nature, enshrined in the metaphorical language of classical metapsychology, picturing mental life in terms of forces, energies, and mechanisms; and an insufficiently critical attitude toward the phenomenological philosophers themselves.

> Many exceptional thinkers have tried to restructure the assumptions of psychoanalysis along phenomenological lines (e.g., Binswanger, 1963; Boss, 1963, 1979; May, Angel, & Ellenberger, 1958). We are in sympathy with such reformulations, insofar as their aim has been to free the phenomenological knowledge of psychoanalysis from its procrustean bed of mechanism and determinism.
>
> (Atwood and Stolorow, 1984, p. 31)

Ludwig Binswanger and Medard Boss, for example, were two early pioneers who saw the value of Heidegger's analysis of existence for psychotherapy and psychoanalysis. They both proceeded "from the top down"—that is, they started with Heidegger's philosophical delineation of essential existential structures and applied these to clinical phenomena and the therapeutic situation. Although Binswanger's (1946) existential analysis produced some brilliant phenomenological descriptions of the "world-designs" (p. 195) underlying various forms of psychopathology,[2] and Boss's (1963) Daseinsanalysis freed the psychoanalytic theory of therapy from the dehumanizing causal-mechanistic assumptions of Freudian metapsychology, neither effort brought about a radicalization of psychoanalytic practice itself or of the psychoanalytic process. The evolution of our own psychoanalytic perspective, by contrast, proceeded "from the bottom up." It was born of our studies of the subjective origins of psychoanalytic theories and developed out of our concurrent efforts to rethink psychoanalysis as a form of phenomenological inquiry and to illuminate the phenomenology of the psychoanalytic process itself.

This relates to the third of the developments in our understanding of the relationship between psychoanalysis and philosophy. The proposals of philosophical phenomenology, we came to realize, arise out of the solitary reflections of individual persons and inevitably embody a particularization of scope associated with the philosopher's personal subjectivity. Husserl's transcendental phenomenology, Heidegger's existential analytic of Dasein, and Sartre's dialectic of being and nothingness each carry the unmistakable signature of their creator's unique personality. The philosophical systems have a metaphysical–ontological core, and, as we had shown to be the case in our studies of the personality theorists in *Faces in a Cloud*, this universalizing core reflects and symbolizes the issues and struggles of the philosopher's personal existence. Analyzing the philosophical thinking in its individual subjective context seemed to be of assistance in clarifying the limits to generality of the philosophical ideas as foundational for a science of experience, and thus in pointing beyond their particular horizons of applicability. We were beginning to see the rich potential of what later we called "the reciprocity between the philosophy of psychoanalysis and the psychoanalysis of philosophy" (Atwood, Stolorow, and Orange, 2011).

6. George Atwood

Commencing in 1980, I taught a seminar for college seniors at Rutgers University entitled "Madness and Creative Genius." This class continued to be offered over a period of 24 years. Each year, my students and I selected a figure from philosophy, literature, or psychology, who engaged in works of great creativity but whose life also showed signs of madness. Our goal in each instance was to understand the relationship between the madness and the genius. Among the many creators we studied were Carl Gustav Jung, Sylvia Plath, Jean-Jacques Rousseau, Franz Kafka, Fyodor Dostoevsky, Rainer Maria Rilke, Virginia Woolf, Jacques Derrida, Heinz Kohut, Søren Kierkegaard, Friedrich Nietzsche, Martin Heidegger, Ludwig Wittgenstein, and Jean-Paul Sartre.

Each study involved an immersion in the most important works of the figure selected and a sustained collaborative effort to relate the major themes of his or her writings to the context of the creator's life history. I regard the influence of these absorbing explorations on my own thinking to have been profound, opening my mind to an ever-expanding and deepening knowledge of creativity and its richly varied linkages to the psychological catastrophes that may occur in a human life. Unexpectedly, my ongoing clinical practice as a psychotherapist interacted powerfully with the research conducted in my seminars. Again and again, I found that what I was learning in my practice working with very severe emotional disturbances was applicable to the studies of the geniuses; correspondingly, insights achieved in the analyses of the creators, I discovered, helped me in understanding my most challenging patients (Atwood, Stolorow, and Orange, 2011).

All of these intellectual journeys were of importance, but possibly the most transforming for me personally and for the continuing shared work with Bob were the studies of Kierkegaard, Nietzsche, Heidegger, Wittgenstein, and Sartre. In 2002, we had discussions about the significance of an understanding of these philosophers for our own continuing efforts to formulate a psychoanalytic phenomenology. Over the decade of the 1990s, we had become aware of the pervasiveness of the doctrine of the Cartesian isolated mind in psychoanalysis. We took the view that this doctrine was a modern myth (Stolorow and Atwood, 1992), to be overcome by an increasingly radical phenomenological-contextualist way of thinking about the nature of psychoanalytic theory and therapy. The particular philosophers listed above were, like us, rebels against Descartes, and we knew we had already been drawing on their thought in our own efforts across the years. An idea came to us that a way of further advancing our own understanding would be to examine these post-Cartesian geniuses psychologically and to identify the personal sources and meanings of their various departures from the Cartesian legacy. It seemed to us that we might use their personal life journeys as a distant mirror in which we could glimpse the meanings of our own passionate quest for a truly post-Cartesian psychoanalysis.

For a decade or more, we tossed around the possibility of such a project and finally it came together in our paper, "The madness and genius of post-Cartesian philosophy: A distant mirror" (Atwood, Stolorow, and Orange, 2011). Drawing on the discoveries that occurred in my seminar, and on years of intensive discussions between us that also included Donna Orange and a collaborative investigation of Heidegger's fall into Nazism (Stolorow, Atwood, and Orange, 2010), here is what we found:

> Each [of the post-Cartesian philosophers] suffered extreme trauma in his personal world, eventuating in a lifelong struggle with profound inner conflict. Their thinking, in addition to being brilliant and innovative, also in each instance embodied an effort to master or otherwise come to terms with persistent emotional tensions presenting the danger of fragmentation. We found madness in the genius of their works, arising from the tragic, disintegrating, and even annihilating conditions dominating their life histories. There were personal demons with which they fought, often ambivalently and with uneven success, and the intellectual journeys for which they are famous dramatically reflect and symbolize their efforts to bring themselves together and emotionally survive.
>
> (Atwood and Stolorow, 2014, p. 111; see also Atwood, 1993)

Gazing into the mirror of the philosophers' life histories, we were then led to reflections on our own demons, on the personal contexts and sources of our interests in developing an embracing phenomenological contextualism.

> Perhaps not surprisingly, we saw more clearly the power of trauma in each of our lives, including experiences of shattering loss, of tyrannical invalidation, and personal fragmentation. We also began to recognize all the ways that intersubjectivity theory constituted a kind of answer to the events and circumstances that had been most difficult. The theory that is our Holy Grail . . . seeks victory over demonic forces that tear us away from ourselves and each other, that confront us with crushing definitions of who we are and

> should be, and that threaten the survival of our very subjectivity as experiencing persons.
>
> (Atwood and Stolorow, 2014, p. 111)

7. Robert Stolorow

My studies in Continental phenomenology, along with further developments of my psychoanalytic perspective, were spurred by terrible personal tragedy.

When the book *Contexts of Being* (Stolorow and Atwood, 1992) was first published, an initial batch of copies was sent "hot-off-the-press" to the display table at a conference where I was a panelist. I picked up a copy and looked around excitedly for my late wife, Dede, who would be so pleased and happy to see it. She was, of course, nowhere to be found, having died some 20 months earlier. I had awakened one morning to find her lying dead across our bed, four weeks after her metastatic cancer had been diagnosed. I spent the remainder of that conference in 1992 remembering and grieving, consumed with feelings of horror and sorrow over what had happened to Dede and to me.

There was a dinner at that conference for all the panelists, many of whom were my old and good friends and close colleagues. Yet, as I looked around the ballroom, they all seemed like strange and alien beings to me. Or, more accurately, *I* seemed like a strange and alien being—not of this world. The others seemed so vitalized, engaged with one another in a lively manner. I, in contrast, felt deadened and broken, a shell of the man I had once been. An unbridgeable gulf seemed to open up, separating me forever from my friends and colleagues. They could never even begin to fathom my experience, I thought to myself, because we now lived in altogether different worlds.

Over the course of six years following that painful occasion, I tried to understand and conceptualize the dreadful sense of estrangement and isolation that seemed to me to be inherent to the experience of emotional trauma. I became aware that this sense of alienation and aloneness appears as a common theme in the trauma literature, and I was able to hear about it from many of my patients who had experienced severe traumatization. One such young man, who had suffered multiple losses of beloved family members during his childhood and adulthood, told me that the world was divided into two groups—the normals and the traumatized ones. There was no possibility, he said, for a normal ever to grasp the experience of a traumatized one. I remembered how important it had been to me to believe that the analyst I saw after Dede's death was also a person who had known devastating loss, and how I implored her not to say anything that could disabuse me of my belief.

How was this experiential chasm separating the traumatized person from other human beings to be understood? In the chapter on trauma that I had written for *Contexts of Being*, I contended that the essence of emotional trauma lay in the experience of unbearable affect and that, developmentally, such intolerability is constituted within an intersubjective system characterized by massive malattunement to the child's emotional pain. In my experience, this conceptualization of developmental trauma as a relational process involving malattunement to painful affect has proven to be of enormous clinical value in the treatment of traumatized patients. Yet, as I began to recognize at that conference dinner, this formulation fails to distinguish between an attunement that cannot be supplied by others and an attunement that cannot be felt by the traumatized person, because of the profound sense of singularity that seemed to me to be built into the experience of trauma itself. A beginning comprehension of this isolating estrangement came from an unexpected source: the philosophical hermeneutics of Hans-Georg Gadamer, whose work I had begun to read.

Concerned as it is with the nature of understanding, philosophical hermeneutics has immediate relevance for the profound despair about having one's experience understood that lies at the heart of emotional trauma. Axiomatic for Gadamer (1975) is the proposition that all understanding involves interpretation. Interpretation, in turn, can only be from a perspective embedded in the historical matrix of the interpreter's own traditions. Understanding, therefore, is always from a perspective whose horizons are delimited by the historicity of the interpreter's organizing principles, by the fabric of preconceptions that Gadamer calls *prejudice*. Gadamer illustrates his hermeneutical philosophy by applying it to the anthropological problem of attempting to understand an alien culture in which the forms of social life, the horizons of experience, are incommensurable with those of the investigator.

At some point while studying Gadamer's work, I recalled my feeling at the conference dinner that I was an alien to the normals around me. The two "hermeneutical situations" seemed analogous to me: I felt as though I lived in a world alien to that of my friends and colleagues. In Gadamer's terms, I felt certain that the horizons of their experience could never encompass mine, and this conviction was the source of my alienation and solitude, of the unbridgeable gulf that I believed separated me from their understanding. It is not just that the traumatized ones and the normals live in different worlds, I thought; it is that these discrepant worlds are felt by the traumatized person to be essentially and ineradicably incommensurable.

Some six years after the conference dinner, I heard something in a lecture delivered by George that helped me to comprehend further the nature of this felt incommensurability. In the course of discussing the clinical implications of an intersubjective contextualism from which Cartesian objectivism had been expunged, George offered a nonobjectivist, dialogic definition of psychotic delusions: "Delusions are ideas whose validity is not open for discussion." This definition fit well with a proposal we had made a dozen years earlier that, when a child's perceptual and emotional experiences meet with massive and consistent invalidation, then his or her belief in the reality of such experiences will remain unsteady and vulnerable to dissolution, and further, that under such predisposing circumstances delusional ideas may develop that "serve to dramatize and reify [an] endangered psychic reality . . . restoring [the] vanishing belief in its validity" (Stolorow, Brandchaft, and Atwood, 1987, p. 133). Delusional ideas were understood as a form of absolutism—a radical decontextualization serving vital restorative and defensive functions. Experiences that are insulated from dialogue cannot be challenged or invalidated.

After hearing George's presentation, I began to think about the role such absolutisms unconsciously play in everyday life. When a person says to a friend, "I'll see you later," or a parent says to a child at bedtime, "I'll see you in the morning," these are statements, like delusions, whose validity is not open for discussion. Such absolutisms are the basis for a kind of naive realism and optimism that allow one to function in the world, experienced as stable, predictable, and safe. It is in the essence of emotional trauma, I concluded, that it shatters these absolutisms, a catastrophic loss of innocence that permanently alters one's sense of being-in-the-world. Massive deconstruction of the absolutisms of everyday life exposes the inescapable contingency of existence on a universe that is chaotic and unpredictable and in which no safety or continuity of being can be assured. Trauma thereby exposes "the unbearable embeddedness of being" (Stolorow and Atwood, 1992, p. 22). As a result, the traumatized person cannot help but perceive aspects of existence that lie well outside the absolutized horizons of normal everydayness. It is in this sense that the worlds of traumatized persons are felt to be fundamentally incommensurable with those of others, the deep chasm in which an anguished sense of estrangement and solitude takes form.

Motivated in part by how beneficial Gadamer's work had been for understanding my traumatized state, I turned at this point to more systematic studies of philosophical texts. In the year 2000, I formed a leaderless philosophical reading group that ran for two years, the first of which was devoted to a close reading of Heidegger's (1927) *Being and Time*. This study of Heidegger proved to be pivotal for me.

Being and Time is an investigation of the meaning of Being. Three aspects of Heidegger's investigation soon stood out for me as holding striking relevance for our evolving psychoanalytic phenomenological contextualism. First was his crucial initial move in choosing the inquirer himself/herself as the entity to be interrogated as to its Being. Heidegger reasoned that, because an unarticulated, pre-philosophical understanding of our Being is constitutive of our kind of Being, we humans can investigate our own kind of Being by investigating our understanding of that Being. Accordingly, the investigative method in *Being and Time* is a *phenomenological* one, aimed at illuminating the fundamental structures of our understanding of our Being. Just as *Faces in a Cloud* begins with our investigations of the personal phenomenologies of psychoanalytic theorists *en route* to a recasting of psychoanalysis as a form of phenomenological inquiry, *Being and Time* begins with the phenomenology of the inquirer *en route* to a claim that ontology is possible only as phenomenology.

Second, Heidegger's ontological contextualism—his mending of the Cartesian subject–object split with the claim that our Being is always already a Being-in-the-world—immediately struck me as providing a solid philosophical grounding for our psychoanalytic contextualism, replacing the Cartesian isolated mind.

Third, and even more important for me at the time, when I read the passages in *Being and Time* devoted to Heidegger's existential analysis of *Angst*, I nearly fell off my chair! Both his phenomenological description and ontological account of *Angst* bore a remarkable resemblance to what I had concluded about the phenomenology and meaning of emotional trauma some two years earlier. In short, Heidegger's analysis of *Angst*, world-collapse, uncanniness, and thrownness into Being-toward-death provided me with extraordinary philosophical tools for grasping the existential significance of emotional trauma. It was this latter discovery that motivated me to begin doctoral studies in philosophy and to write a dissertation and two books (Stolorow 2007, 2011) on Heidegger and what George and I had come to call *post-Cartesian psychoanalysis*. My dual aim in this work was to show both how Heidegger's existential philosophy enriches post-Cartesian psychoanalysis and how post-Cartesian psychoanalysis enriches Heidegger's existential philosophy.

8. George Atwood and Robert Stolorow—The phenomenological circle

In the course of our love affairs with philosophy we have sought to refashion psychoanalysis as a phenomenological contextualism that investigates and illuminates worlds of emotional experience, the structures prereflectively organizing them, and the intersubjective contexts in which these structures take form. Such refashioning, in turn, has led us inexorably to a deconstructive critique of psychoanalytic metapsychologies (Atwood and Stolorow, 2014, Chapter 8).

We have concluded that psychoanalytic metapsychologies are actually a form of metaphysics, and we have elaborated upon a claim first introduced by Wilhelm Dilthey that metaphysics represents an illusory flight from the tragedy of human finitude. Metaphysics transforms the unbearable fragility and transience of all things human into an enduring, permanent, changeless reality, an illusory world of eternal truths. Using the work and lives of philosophers and psychoanalytic theorists as illustrative "clinical" cases, we have contended that the best safeguard against the pitfalls of metaphysical illusion lies in a shared commitment to reflection upon the phenomenological underpinnings and constitutive contexts of origin of all our theoretical ideas. The growth of our theoretical understanding thus follows an endlessly recurring *phenomenological circle*, joining theoretical perspectives with the inquirers from whose emotional worlds they arise.

Reflection and context

In our continuing efforts to explore and illuminate the philosophical assumptions and personal foundations of our proposals for a psychoanalytic phenomenology, we were led to a series of questions.

One of the tasks to be faced in the continuing development of phenomenological contextualism is that of reflecting upon the process of reflection itself.

One may ask a number of interrelated questions. What exactly is reflection? What are reflection's constitutive contexts? What are the constitutive contexts of the idea of a context itself? What precisely is a "context," and what is meant by describing it as "constitutive"? And how do these various issues and our responses to them relate to our own lives and personal subjectivity? In posing such questions, we continue to circle back on our own personal and philosophical foundations.

Here are some of the thoughts that were raised by the posing of these questions:

1. The act of psychoanalytic reflection is always a contextualization. Any experience or action brought into reflective awareness is seen against a certain background of elements in relation to which it is given meaning. That background is the context and forms a grouping of which what is being reflected upon is viewed as a part.
2. Consider the case of interpreting a dream, using the dreamer's associations to the dream imagery as aids in deciphering initially hidden meanings. By placing the dream's manifest content within an array of associated thoughts, feelings, and memories, the initially opaque dream experience may be rendered transparent as an organic expression of the dreamer's subjective life.
3. A constitutive context is a grouping of elements participating in the very being of the object of psychoanalytic reflection. A constitutive context is a part of the world to which that object belongs.
4. There may be more than one context that is constitutive.
5. Identifying the constitutive context(s) of a person's experiences and actions reunites them with his or her world and overcomes the isolating and fragmenting effects of decontextualization. Inasmuch as personal existence is irreducibly relational and contextual, decontextualization is always also depersonalization. An essential—perhaps *the* essential—feature of psychoanalytic therapy is the recontextualization and therefore the repersonalization of the patient's suffering.
6. One of the constitutive contexts of our emphasis on the central importance of reflection is historical and philosophical, residing in the influence on our thinking of the efforts of the great phenomenological philosophers to bring into reflective awareness the universal structures of human experience. Our concern with personal organizing principles and the critical formative events out of which they crystallize in the life history of the individual is a kind of counterpart to the philosophers' focus on the preconditions and prereflective organization of experience in general.
7. Another constitutive context of our focus on the discovery of the constitutive contexts illuminated by psychoanalytic reflection is one of very severe trauma in our own personal lives, resulting then in persistent efforts to overcome shattering loss, isolation, and corrosive invalidation.
8. ?—to be continued.

Notes

1 Chapters with no author listed beneath the title have been written by both George E. Atwood and Robert D. Stolorow.

2 In subsequent not-yet-translated work, summarized by Stolorow (2011, p. 73) with the help of translations by Roger Frie (personal communication), Binswanger, drawing especially on the thinking of Martin Buber, sought to supplement Heidegger's rather thin account of authentic relationality.

2

SEEDS OF PSYCHOANALYTIC PHENOMENOLOGY

A formative clinical experience

George E. Atwood

From 1969 to 1972, I was a Post-Doctoral Fellow in Clinical Psychology at the Western Missouri Mental Health Center in Kansas City. I was drawn to this institution because of its Director of Clinical Training, the legendary psychotherapist Austin Des Lauriers, author of *The Experience of Reality in Childhood Schizophrenia* (1962). In that book, he argued that so-called schizophrenia consists, at its core, of a catastrophic loss of the sense of the real. Its psychotherapy, accordingly, involves most centrally the reconsolidation and restoration of that sense. Although Des Lauriers made use of medical-diagnostic language in his writings, his fundamental conception was about something happening in subjective experience—i.e., it was phenomenological. Looking back, it seems to me that working closely with him infused a lasting phenomenological spirit into my thinking. His influence was most dramatically and fatefully transmitted in his supervision of my work with a patient who believed she was God. In what follows, I tell the story of that patient and her therapy.

The patient who thought she was the Holy Ghost

I first met the patient to be described when she arrived at the screening clinic of the mental health center where I was being trained one morning at 3 am. Brought to the hospital by her mother and brother, her eyes were wide with excitement, perspiration drenched her clothes, and she was shouting and carrying on. She cried out that she needed to see someone important. I presented myself as that important person and sat down to hear her story. There had been multiple flashes of golden light in and around her home, she explained, and the flashes had come into her bedroom and penetrated her body. She said: "They filled me up and I was going to BUST!" I asked her to tell me what she thought this golden energy was. She answered: "I had sexual intercourse with Jesus Christ!"

The patient, whom I shall call Grace, 28 years old, was admitted to the inpatient service and one of our psychiatrists gave her the diagnosis: schizophrenia, paranoid type—DSM-II: 295.3. She was well-qualified for this diagnosis, seen from a purely medical point of view: clear signs of thought disorder, inappropriate affect, visual hallucinations, delusions of grandeur. I, however, was interested from the beginning not in her diagnosis but in understanding her strange and amazing ideas. I went to see her the next day following her admission and offered to be her primary therapist. She consented to the proposal.

I saw Grace every day for the next two weeks and then began to consult with Des Lauriers. During these early meetings, she spoke almost entirely about religious matters. I tried to show interest and listened attentively as she went on at great length.

One topic she spent hours speaking about concerned the history of the Catholic Church and what she saw as a tragic distortion in its portrayal of the figure of Jesus Christ. "Jesus was human and real," she loudly exclaimed, "and not just a remote divine essence. He suffered pain, He felt alone, He was betrayed. He was a Man, He was Human, He was not just God!" She seemed to regard it as her personal destiny to correct this historical one-sidedness of Catholic doctrine, to restore to Jesus His human dimension. I asked her if she had read *The Last Temptation of Christ* by Nikos Kazantzakis (1955), which has an idea like hers as its theme. She answered she only read prayer books and the Bible.

A second topic in these early contacts concerned a special relationship she claimed to have with officials in the Church in Rome, including the Pope himself. The College of Cardinals she believed were, as we spoke, deliberating about her canonization, and she awaited their proclamation of her sainthood. She said she knew the Holy Father personally and had on more than one occasion magically flown through the sky to visit him in the Vatican. There had been compelling visions of having floated down from above, alighting at the Pope's side or even on his lap.

A third preoccupation was with the Holy Trinity: God the Father, God the Son, and the Holy Spirit. "They are three," she cried out, "and they are One!" God the Father, she told me, had been miraculously incarnated in the Bishop of her Diocese, and God the Son had appeared in the person of a psychotherapist she had seen and been very attached to during her late teen years. Grace herself embodied the Holy Spirit. When I asked her how she could know such things, she arose from her chair and shouted: "I am the Way, I am the Truth, I am the Light!" She was telling me that she was God. I had never met anyone like this and I had no idea what to do with her. So, I turned to Austin Des Lauriers, and he showed me a way.

When I finally sat down with him and described what I had seen and heard from Grace in our initial meetings, he expressed little interest in the details of her many religious delusions and hallucinations. About all that, he simply said: "Well, she's talking to you. That is good—it gives you a beginning. Be happy that she is actually wanting to talk to you." I then asked what I should say back to her in the face of her preoccupations. Des Lauriers responded with questions: "How is she dressed? What are her clothes like? Her shoes? How does she fix her hair, or does she? With all you are telling me, I doubt if she pays much attention to her appearance." I described to him then how she appeared—she wore raggedy old sneakers, faded jeans, and an old sweatshirt—plus her hair was usually uncombed and kind of all over the place.

> Perfect [Des Lauriers said] because although she pays no attention to how she looks, you can show her that you do. Tell her that her raggedy sneakers are magnificent, compliment her on her old sweatshirt. Show a sparkle of humor and friendliness in your eyes as you talk to her. Maybe you could bring out a comb and stand with her before a mirror, helping her make her hair look nice. Kid around with her about this, maybe combing your own hair.

He explained further that the purpose in all this was to establish myself as a concrete bodily presence in her world, a human being existing in time and space, physically distinct from her but relating to her in an impactful way. The hope was that in such interventions a bond could begin to form that would facilitate the stabilization of her reality and lead eventually to her recovery.

I asked Des Lauriers whether she might experience all this talk about her appearance and her body as a sexual seduction, and if she did, what was I to do about that? I was thinking about her experiences of golden light and her claim to have had sexual intercourse with Jesus Christ. I remember the essence of his reply:

> Don't worry about that at all. This young woman is in the midst of a catastrophe beyond imagining. The experiences she is having are about something far more fundamental than sexuality. You have to use everything you have and everything you are to reach her. You are male and she is female, and her awareness of this difference may have a role to play in the reclaiming of her identity as a person, as a woman. If sexuality somehow becomes an issue down the line, you will deal with it then. It is the least of your worries at this point.

I then returned to my daily meetings with Grace and tried to implement what Des Lauriers was suggesting. When she launched into long disquisitions about the history of the Catholic Church and its one-sided theology, I listened to her but then responded by making comments about her raggedy tennis shoes. I was surprised by her initial reaction—she laughed when I told her the shoes were magnificent, and seemed not to mind having been interrupted. When she began to speak about the goings on at the Vatican and among the Cardinals, I told her she had beautiful blue eyes. Again, she smiled and almost seemed to lap up my admiring words. As she began to hold forth about the Trinity, I told her to stand up and look at herself in the mirror as we stood next to each other. I combed her hair then, remarking on its nice light brown color. Then I combed my own hair before the mirror and asked her if she thought I needed a haircut. I parted it down the middle and inquired as to whether I looked good, or like one of the Three Stooges. Still again, she laughed. I took her for a number of short walks on the hospital grounds, and interrupted her streaming religious fantasies by stopping at a small pond and touching the water. It was very cold and I asked her to feel it. When she held back, I splashed a little in her face, and then apologized. She laughed for a moment, but then returned to her thoughts about Jesus Christ having been both a man and not just God. When she came into my office and I noticed a scratch or a bruise on her arm, I made a big fuss over it and told her that her skin was beautiful and she should be very careful to protect it. Sometimes I made a production out of retrieving a Band-Aid from the nurse's station and applying it to her wound. This last intervention seemed like a good idea in that it might, I thought, strengthen her sense of the bodily boundaries of her own selfhood by drawing her attention away from the streaming of her religious fantasies. It often appeared to me that she was lost in her imagination and experiencing a near-merger with the cosmos as a whole.

So that is what it was like in the early months of our meetings. I saw her 5–7 days a week, most often for an hour or more, and continued to listen to her many thoughts and fantasies. In keeping with Des Lauriers's consultations, I interspersed into her long discussions on religious matters my own remarks and reactions, redirecting her attention to our concrete situation of being with one another physically in space, meeting at our appointed times, Monday through Friday and sometimes on the weekends. He suggested I make a big deal out of the timing of our sessions—which created a contrast to her imagined dwelling in the realm of Eternity. I don't want it to sound like I was constantly interrupting Grace—I was not. I listened patiently for dozens of hours as she held forth at great length, and tried my best to understand what she was saying. Much of the time I could not follow her as she flooded me with her fantasies, and many of our sessions were extremely difficult and exhausting for me. There were however repeating themes. I saw that she was enjoying our contacts and looking forward to them every day. She was always the first to greet me when I arrived at the hospital in the morning, and she was the last to say goodbye at night. In addition, she began to bring me paintings as gifts. Some of these she had completed in the art program at our hospital, but others she asked to be brought from home by her mother. These were chiefly concerned with religious themes: the Holy Virgin, the Crucifixion, the Resurrection. But there were a number of others that seemed more abstract: images of fire, with the words "I AM PAIN," "I AM ANGER," or simply "I AM," scrawled across the canvases in large capital letters. I accepted these gifts and told her I would protect and treasure them. She did not want to discuss her paintings; she just wanted me to have them. The thought occurred to me that in giving me her art, she was entrusting her soul to me for safekeeping. I did not say this to her however—I was too busy talking about her tennis shoes.

The history

Let me now say a few things about her history. Des Lauriers never showed much interest in her background and did not encourage detailed explorations of events from long ago. His clinical experience had taught him that psychoanalytic inquiries into life history were of no value in the psychotherapy of so-called psychosis, and his approach was accordingly oriented throughout to working in the here and now, addressing the ongoing catastrophes of the present. I however wanted to know what had happened in Grace's life to bring her to the state in which I found her. There were short intervals in our early conversations when she showed a lucidity and so I was able, over the course of time, to assemble a narrative about her childhood development. Some of the details and reflections provided in what follows also came from many discussions I had with her years later, following her recovery. Other parts of the account derive from thoughts I have had about my journey with Grace long after our work was completed.

She was one of three children in an Irish Catholic family, with two brothers, raised by her mother and father. Describing herself as always having been an anxious child, she said her mother was cold and harshly disciplinary, but her father was warm and loving. She had numerous memories of sitting on his lap, of helping him with chores around the house, of waiting eagerly for him in the afternoons when he came home from work, and of being comforted by him when she was beaten up by her brothers or disturbed by bad dreams in the night. Her mother during her early years she remembered only as someone who criticized and punished her.

When Grace was 10 years old, her father fell into an unexplained severe depression. She recounted how her mother pleaded with him to get dressed in the mornings and go to work, but how on most days he refused and stayed in bed. Her mother also tried to arrange for him to go for counseling, but this help too he resisted. His deepening depression was broken only by sudden rages, violent outbursts in which he shouted and cursed and threw objects against the wall. Grace said: "When my father exploded I felt the world was coming to an end!" Afraid for her father and her family, she prayed for things to improve. Finally, a morning came when he was much better, almost euphoric in fact, and she thought her prayers were being answered. Later that day he left the house, slashed his wrists, and hanged himself.

"A dark cloud descended on the family," Grace said, "and there was a wall of silence." No one told her what had happened to her father, and she only learned of his death and its circumstances two days later, by reading an account of it in the newspaper. Everyone was devastated, but no one spoke a word about what had occurred. The father was buried without a funeral and his name was not mentioned aloud in the home for the next several years. It seemed to me, judging from Grace's account, that her family had made an effort to act as though the father had never existed in the first place. The most important person in Grace's world, I thought, had thereby been relegated to the effective status of someone who had never been.

Her mother, in the aftermath of the suicide, fell into her own dark depression, going to bed and telling her children that she was soon to die. She warned them that they would now have to fend for themselves. Grace described what her mother was like at that time, in the following words, shouted out: "My mother closed up like gates crashing shut!" There had been a double abandonment, without question, and an attack on her personal reality of the first magnitude.

Such was the context of the next step in Grace's journey: the formation of a special relationship, conducted in secret prayer, with Jesus Christ. She imagined and made herself believe she had a direct channel to Jesus, whose divine love she pictured as filling up the vast emptiness created by the tragic developments in her family. She subsequently also imagined that she could somehow transmit His healing powers to others, including, at the time, a close friend she had met in school who was ill with cancer. Grace poured energy into her prayers on behalf of her friend's recovery—but the girl died. Words formed in her mind: "Jesus Christ abandoned me!" Telling no one of her suffering, she was thrown into a further hidden agony of doubt and loss.

Finally, Grace, now in her teens, resolved her crisis by persuading herself that it was not that Jesus had abandoned her; it was that she had failed to merit His love owing to her own imperfections. A pathway opened up before her young life: one leading to spiritual perfection and purity within herself, and in consequence an eventual spiritual union with her Savior. As a way of carrying her intention through in action, she resolved to become a nun and a missionary, and to devote her life to helping people in need around the world. Her commitment was to a life of utter selflessness, sacrificing and suppressing any and all longings for anything for herself. This included the whole of her emerging sexuality.

Grace entered a convent at age 17, but only lasted a year before emotionally collapsing. Again, the terrible words formed in her mind: "Jesus Christ abandoned me!" She told me what she felt after leaving the convent: an inner deadness, something she dealt with by drinking herself into oblivion every night for the next months. At her mother's urging, she finally went to her priest at her church and asked for a referral for counseling. She was given the name of a psychologist, himself Catholic and well-known in the community for working with emotionally troubled nuns and priests, and a three-year relationship began between them. Grace saw her counselor once each week. He immediately became the center of gravity of her life and she never missed an appointment. I asked her if she told him about her secret channel to Jesus, and about the shattering losses she had experienced in her father's death and in the years following it. She said she did not, these things remaining completely secret. She was utterly impressed by her counselor's gentleness and warmth, and, with his encouragement, applied for a part-time position in the office of the Bishop of her diocese. I asked her what they talked about during her counseling sessions. She answered that they spoke of everyday events mostly, her work for the Bishop, her life with her mother and brothers. He also spoke at length of his work for the Church and for a number of charity organizations to which he devoted much of his life.

As time passed, a dismaying sexual intensity began to color Grace's feelings for her beloved therapist. She was deeply ashamed of her longings and kept them to herself. This man seemed so pure and good, and here she was wishing for erotic contact with him. The actual content of their discussions, as best I was able to gather, increasingly shifted toward him speaking about his own life and work, his own personal struggles, with Grace offering her emotional support to him. There were two currents, deeply conflicting and confusing, that then began to flow in her unspoken inner life. One of these issued from a sense of not being understood by her therapist, of things he said not making sense, of abandonment. The other current was of being in the presence of someone entirely Holy.

It finally came to her that she was indeed with her Lord and Savior Himself. But here she was also feeling desolate and abandoned. Perhaps in an effort to communicate something of her confusion to him, she brought in a series of drawings of strange geometric figures: lines, triangles, rectangles, irregular polygons. Grace was unable to tell me why she had chosen such images—I thought to myself the figures symbolized a failing effort to make order out of chaos, sense out of an intensifying emotional situation that made no sense at all. Her therapist had no comment on her art and showed no awareness of her worsening state.

Finally, near the end of the third year of counseling, she interrupted their session one day by rising from her chair and screaming out: "JESUS CHRIST ABANDONED ME!" She said his jaw dropped in surprise, he mumbled out words to the effect that Jesus had not abandoned her, and she marched out of his office never to return. A few days later, she was hospitalized for the first time, following a violent episode of breaking mirrors and dishes in her home and shouting about God. I read her psychiatric records from this first hospitalization and saw that all the major features of her religious delusions and preoccupations were already present. No effort was made by her therapist to have further contact with her.

Thus began her adventures in psychiatric treatment. In the ensuing period, Grace had a dozen or more separate admissions to the inpatient service in a local community mental health center. The stays in the hospital ranged from weeks to months in duration, always following the same pattern. She would become overwhelmed with hallucinations and religious delusions and become disruptive in her home where she lived with her mother and one of her brothers, hospitalization would occur, sometimes with the help of the police, she would be medicated, and after a variable period the delusions would recede and she would be discharged. And so it went for the next eight years, until she and I found each other.

A transformational moment

My experience of working with Grace in the early months of our relationship was one of riding a volcano. I saw her almost every day. Although our meetings sometimes seemed to calm her and enable her to talk rationally and coherently for brief periods, periodically she would erupt with religious fantasies and shout them to the heavens. Once, she burst in upon a game of pool I was playing with another patient and pushed the two of us away. Then she picked up the cue ball and held it high in the air, crying out: "This is the Holy Ghost!" Then she slammed the ball down on the pool table and shot it at the other balls with great force. She seemed pleased when a number of the other balls flew off the table. Another time she interrupted a bingo game I was conducting for depressed ladies. She took center stage and began to spin around and scream: "I am cured! I am healed! I am saved! And who is it that is my Savior? That man, Dr. Atwood! Whoopee!" On still another occasion I arrived in the early morning to find her walking dramatically about the floor in the hospital, arm in arm with a man who entertained the idea that he was God. Grace saw me come in, and called out: "We are married, Doctor, in the eyes of Christ!"

There was a ferocious intensity in Grace's claims, a kind of omnipotence that seemed to know no limits, an omniscient certainty that was never to be questioned. Des Lauriers continued to support my doing whatever I could to bring our interactions down to the most concrete of levels, but the passion of her religiosity only seemed to be increasing. I remember going to him after a number of months and asking him: "How long in the face of a woman engaged with God can I talk about her tennis shoes?" I remember him laughing but then asking me for a more complete description of her expressions. I gave him a detailed fresh account of what she was saying and doing, all of it centering on her relationship to God. That relationship included the central idea that she was, by virtue of the mystery of the Holy Trinity, herself God. Des Lauriers then said: "She is really a sick girl, isn't she?"

As we went along in our daily meetings, she now seemed to me to be getting worse rather than better. My continuing interventions emphasizing our concrete situation with each other, as Des Lauriers had recommended, seemed increasingly to go nowhere, and her passionate expressions about God were intensifying. I began to feel like tearing my hair out.

Grace at this point informed me of a secret that she had hitherto kept concealed. She said: "Doctor, there is something I have not told you. I am going to tell you now. I have been working on something for two years: a Plan." I asked her then: "What plan? A plan for what?" Her answer, shouted: "MY PLAN TO REACH MY GOLD!" At first, I did not understand, and asked: "Your goal?" She responded with a roar: "MY GOALLLLLLLLLDDDDD!" It was then explained. For the previous two years, Grace had been conducting a special program of meditation and prayer designed to transform the world, bring peace to conflicting nations, solve all the Earth's problems, and bring on the Second Coming or Christ and the End of Times. The word "GOLD" condensed two ideas: "goal" and "God." It was the precise goal of her striving to become one with God. There had also been the flashes of GOLDEN light that came to her in the night and penetrated into her body.

Executing this Plan involved something more. Once the meditations had begun to take effect, there was to be a meeting between Grace and her former therapist, a reunion that then the Bishop would also join. A merger of the three could then take place, and an Ascension into Heaven as the Trinity burst forth in radiant glory. She told me that I had an important role in this: I was to call her former therapist and arrange the meeting with him that would be the prelude to the Ascension. "I know I can count on you to call him and arrange for our meeting, Dr. Atwood. Call him. Now!" I was uneasy with this instruction, and unable to foresee what would happen in such a reunion. I told her I was not sure this was a good idea. She screamed in response: "You will do it! If you want to know me and be a part of my life, you will participate in my Plan and follow all my instructions regarding it! So do it! Now! My time has come!"

I told Grace I would give her my answer the next day and somehow managed to extricate myself from our meeting. I left her still shouting at me. Then I called Des Lauriers and arranged a special consultation with him. He listened as I described this conversation and I remember him frowning as I gave an account of Grace's Plan and her instructions regarding my role in carrying it out. He then said:

> There is all this talk about her plan. What about your plan for her? Your plan is that she is to get well and be able to return home and live with the people who love her. The only meetings that need to be arranged are the ones between you and her. I think, George, it is time for you to rise and shine. You have to go toe-to-toe, mano-a-mano, and fight fire with fire. I think she may, contrary to appearances, be seeking a strength outside herself that she can finally count on after so many years of abandonment. Go home and think about what you can say to her tomorrow.

That night I was so worried about what the next day would bring. I had never opposed anything Grace had said, and I did not kow what to anticipate from her if I now assumed a different attitude with her. By this time, I had spent upwards of 150 hours with her, being receptive, patient, and friendly throughout. I dreamt that night that I was married to her—a terrible nightmare marriage from which there could be no escape.

I met with Grace the next afternoon, and our session took an entirely different course, for both of us. When she arrived, I saw she was ready to resume talk of her Plan, but before she could even begin I asked her to wait and listen to something important that I had to say to her. She shouted I was "cutting her off!" I answered: "No, it is you who are doing the cutting off at this point. I have listened to you carefully for days and weeks and months, and I need you now to be quiet and listen." Finally, she stopped talking. Here is what I then said, in a calm but firm voice:

> There has been a lot of talk about a Plan. I want you to know that I now have a Plan for you, and in my Plan you are going to get well and be able to return home from the hospital and live with the people who love you.

> In terms of any meetings to be arranged, there is only one person on this planet you need to be concerned with meeting. I am that person. It will be in our work together that my Plan for you will be followed up and be successful. I need you to take what I am saying in. It is up to you and to me, and no one else.

Grace tried to interrupt me several times as I presented this little statement, but I stopped her in each instance and held my ground. I had to repeat myself perhaps three times in somewhat different words. Finally, she was silent, and then she began to cry. We were well into our seventh month of our meetings, and I had never seen her cry before this moment. She cried and cried, and then she cried some more. The crying went on for twenty minutes or more, and then stopped. She said just two words, "Thank you," and then she left my office.

I remember worrying that night about the impact of the confrontation we had just undergone. Would Grace kill herself? Would she grow worse than ever and disappear into the madness? When I arrived the next morning, I found she was not in the hospital—she had somehow prevailed upon the staff to release her for the day on a visit home. I called her home to see what was going on, fearing I would learn she was on the roof screaming to the Heavens about the Second Coming.

I reached Grace's mother, and here is what she said:

> Dr. Atwood, what did you do? Grace came home this morning and she is herself again! She sat down with me on our porch for tea and asked me about the latest gossip about our neighbors! She talked about wanting to help me take care of our house. She even mentioned she wanted to get a job again! Dr. Atwood, this is a miracle!

Later that day, Grace returned from her home visit and she and I sat down to talk. I found her completely transformed. She spoke to me excitedly about having enjoyed her visit with her mother and about her future when she left the hospital, including some ideas about getting a job and helping her mother out financially in maintaining their home. She was rational, coherent, not at all religiously preoccupied, completely sane. As an apparent result of a 30-minute meeting with me the day before, her so-called psychosis had vanished, without a trace. After witnessing this astonishing transformation, I have never been able to see psychosis in the same way. One needs to have experiences such as this one in order to learn what is and is not possible through psychotherapy.

A few days later, I met with Des Lauriers and described what had happened in the fateful 30-minute meeting with Grace, and the resulting change that had occurred in her condition. He was happy that I had followed his suggestion and liked the way I had implemented it. He told me a few stories of similar crisis points that he had experienced in the therapy of the most severe psychological disturbances, with parallel remarkable effects. He also mentioned a famous comedy routine of Shelley Berman that my confrontation with Grace reminded him of. In that hilarious routine, the comedian gave an account of trying to reach his sister when the phone was answered by her very young son, his nephew. The little boy basically played games with his uncle, teasing him, refusing to give the phone to his mother, acting silly, even hanging up and having to be called back a time or two. This went on and on, endlessly, frustratingly for Shelley Berman, until finally he shouted to the boy: "THIS IS GOD! GIVE ME YOUR MOTHER!" The boy, now scared out of his wits, complied.

I was able recently to locate a YouTube recording of this funny story. In it, Shelley Berman not only says that he is God, he tells his nephew that, if he does not immediately give the phone to his mother, lightning will strike the boy and he will be burned to the ground! I made no such threats against Grace, and I also did not claim to be God. But I did push my own Plan to help her become well again, and in effect pushed back hard against her long-standing, driving agenda to bring on the End of the World and become one with her God in Heaven. She not only accepted what I was offering to her; she embraced it like a drowning person grabbing on to a life preserver. Des Lauriers thought this was what she had been asking and reaching for all along.

Did the "miracle" of Grace's transformation last? No. In the ensuing weeks, she fell back several times, again becoming consumed by the religious fantasies and delusions. In each instance I had to repeat my little spiel about the centrality of our work together in following the pathway of her healing. Each time this occurred, however, it was easier, and after two months all references to her former religious preoccupations vanished, never to return.

Looking back over the following two years of my continuing psychotherapy with Grace, two things stand out in my memory. First, her dependence was initially extreme. If I was late for one of our meetings, even by just a few minutes, I found her reduced to abject terror. She also often remarked on what a powerful person I had become in her life, occasionally telling me I possessed a profound spiritual quality. Reading between the lines, it seemed to me she was experiencing me as a kind of God-figure. I chose not to respond to such attributions directly, because I thought she was using our connection to reassemble a shattered personal universe. A second development that appeared as her recovery continued pertained to Grace's long-deferred emotional reactions to her father's suicide. She spoke at length about his death to her mother and brothers, and for months wept bitterly about the tragedy. Feelings of deep rage at him for deliberately ending his life also surfaced during this period, and she wondered if she could ever forgive him for choosing to die. She was angry not only for herself, but also for her brothers and especially her mother, who had almost been destroyed by the suicide.

My psychotherapeutic sessions with Grace continued until the end of our third year, after which I saw or spoke to her only once a month or less. We remained in touch however for the next three decades, exchanging birthday and Christmas greetings. Grace was a faithful Catholic and attended Mass almost every day, working part-time in a secretarial capacity for her church and living with her mother and brother. She was a joy to them both. She also loved animals and was instrumental in the ensuing years in rescuing many dogs and cats. Grace died at the age of 59, of a sudden cardiac infarction. This was immensely sad, because she was one of the finest people I have ever known.

Dialogue

RDS: This is a great clinical story, George, vividly describing events that I know have had a lasting impact on you. In your introductory remarks, you say that working with your beloved Des Lauriers "infused" you with a phenomenological spirit. Can you say more about that? How exactly did he transmit this influence?

GEA: I had read Des Lauriers's (1962) book, *The Experience of Reality in Childhood Schizophrenia*, before I met him, and I had seen that it was about experience most centrally, in spite of its use of medical-diagnostic terminology. I recall feeling a powerful resonance to its underlying message, which is all about a kind of cataclysm that occurs in subjectivity, and about what is required of a psychotherapeutic relationship in order for a restoration to occur. The resonance was so strong that it came into my mind that I might have written his book myself, or that I could become capable of having written it following more years of clinical experience. Its pathways of thought seemed oddly familiar, as if I had read it before, as if he had taken a collection of my half-formed, fragmentary intuitions and extended and deepened them into an elegant structure. Looking back, I think I was responding to his underlying phenomenology.

RDS: And yet, he writes of "schizophrenia," a non-phenomenological, actually anti-phenomenological diagnostic concept. It is confusing.

GEA: Yes, it is confusing, and I think it is so because it is itself confused. If you think about it, Des Lauriers's masterwork's title is virtually oxymoronic: it speaks of Experience—which is phenomenological—and it speaks of Schizophrenia—which is diagnostic and anti-phenomenological. I had conversations with him in the mid-1970s in which this came up. He told me he had deliberately made use of diagnostic language in an effort to reach out to the broader psychiatric community and spread his ideas and discoveries. His book also employs a lot of terminology from psychoanalytic ego psychology, and this too he chose in order to find contact with the psychoanalytic world. He said these decisions had probably been mistakes, because the language used ended up obscuring the underlying phenomenological message and its powerful therapeutic implications. I now think of Austin Des Lauriers as a transitional figure in the evolution of a consistently phenomenological contextualism applied to extreme states involving a sense of personal annihilation. It's kind of sad, because he was a complete genius and I worshipped the ground he walked on.

RDS: We'll take up the issue of diagnostic language in a later chapter. Regarding Grace, do you think that Grace experienced a sense of personal annihilation—or better, a collapse of her emotional world—in reaction to her father's suicide? Did she try to resurrect him and her world in her preoccupations with God and Jesus Christ? Did she need to resurrect him in you instead? Did Des Lauriers sense that without explicitly naming it when he told you it was time for you to *rise and shine*?

GEA: Grace's father's suicide, along with her family's turning away from his death and life, was a savage blow against her world. She had believed her father loved her, but how could he have, in view of his having deliberately chosen to die? He had been emotionally central to her; but, in the absolute silence following his death, it was as if he had been erased, relegated to the status of someone who never was. These twin invalidations, I think, attacked everything she believed in. I see her turning to Jesus Christ as an effort to resurrect a collapsing personal reality by replacing her father with the God she believed would never leave her. This function of solidifying Grace's world eventually passed over on to me, without question, along with the terror of abandonment arising out of her massive history of trauma. Des Lauriers saw clearly the necessity that I assume unequivocal centrality in the restoration of her shattered universe.

RDS: Devastating loss entailing a collapse of one's emotional world and a quest for its resurrection—I know that you are all-too-familiar with this theme yourself, George. Perhaps this speaks to how deeply you could relate to Grace's experience and also to how you worshipped Des Lauriers. Talk to me about all that, please.

GEA: Actually, Grace and her tragedy opened me up to my own shattering experience of loss. Before she appeared in my life, I was largely unaware of how deeply I too had been affected by the loss of a beloved parent during childhood—the sudden death of my mother when I was 8 years old. Seeing Grace contend with the emotional devastation wrought by her father's killing himself released in gradual stages my own arrested mourning. There was an additional parallel between her response to tragedy and my own: both of us had adopted a rescuing attitude in our lives, based in identifications with our lost idealized parents. My dawning awareness of this parallel was involved in a series of papers I wrote very early in my career, including one that was our first collaborative essay, "Messianic projects and early object relations" (Stolorow and Atwood, 1973; Atwood, 1978). Both of us, I saw, had resurrected our lost worlds by becoming saviors of others. I was able to relate quite profoundly to Grace's experience of loss, but I could not do so without discovering my own buried grief. As you know, the story of George Atwood's loss of his mother and its lasting impact on his life and thought is told in a chapter of the second edition of our book, *Structures of Subjectivity* (Atwood and Stolorow, 2014), entitled "The demons of phenomenological contextualism."

I am not sure how any of this pertains to my hero-worship of Des Lauriers, although I am sure that it must. There were a number of other challenging clinical cases in which consultations with him led to breakthroughs that I could not imagine happening without his input. He always seemed to understand the situations I presented to him, and to know exactly what to do. The pattern was repeatedly the same: I would become entangled with a severely disturbed patient, a crisis would occur in the therapy, I would run to Des Lauriers and receive the golden words, and I would then implement his advice and a resolution of the crisis would occur. What took place with Grace was a special case of a general pattern. He saw quite clearly how much I was learning from him, and how he had become a powerful mentor in my development as a psychotherapist. He was completely accepting and told me he had experienced the same thing early in his training.

RDS: What about my earlier question regarding whether Grace experienced a sense of personal annihilation? I suggested a better description of what she felt was a collapse of her emotional world. Is the collapse of a world the same thing as the annihilation of one's selfhood, or is there a difference between the two?

GEA: In the final chapter of our book, *Worlds of Experience* (Stolorow, Atwood, and Orange, 2002), I discussed this question as follows:

> Experiences of self and world are inextricably bound up with one another, in the sense that any dramatic change in the one necessarily involves a corresponding change in the other. Self-dissolution, for example, is not a subjective event that could leave the world of the individual otherwise intact, with the selfhood of the person somehow subtracted out. The experience of self-loss means the loss of an enduring center in relation to which the totality of the individual's experiences is organized. The dissolution of one's selfhood thus produces an inevitable disintegrating effect on the person's experience in general, and results in the loss of coherence of the world itself. Likewise, the breakup of the unity of the world means the loss of a stable reality in relation to which the sense of self is defined and sustained, and an experience of self-fragmentation inevitably follows in its wake. World-disintegration and self-dissolution are thus inseparable aspects of a single process, two faces of the same psychological catastrophe.
>
> (p. 148)

I remember presenting the story of Grace in a seminar conducted by Des Lauriers shortly after my work with her commenced, still many months before we had our breakthrough. In formulating her subjective situation at this early stage, I said in my presentation that I thought there was no "ego" present in her world, that the sense of "I" was somehow strangely missing in the swirling of her fantasies and delusions about Jesus Christ and the Holy Trinity. Des Lauriers told me he found my formulation extremely interesting. I also think of the many paintings she gave me in those early days of our relationship, particularly of the representations of a consuming fire with the words "I AM PAIN," "I AM ANGER," or just "I AM," scrawled across the canvases in large capital letters. Such creations seemed to me to unequivocally express a surging protest against a sense of having been erased and annihilated.

RDS: You characterized Des Lauriers's influence on you as an "infusion" of phenomenological understanding and as a receiving of his "golden words," followed by their implementation. Grace introduced herself to you after an infusion of the "golden light" of Jesus Christ into her body, which she further said was "sexual intercourse." What do you make of this parallelism? The theme in common is an incorporative identification with an idealized parental figure. Is this commonality an example of what we have called an *intersubjective conjunction* between your two emotional worlds?

GEA: My answer to your question is an unequivocal "Yes." Sometimes, I have the impression that the healing process of psychotherapy always and necessarily involves a parallelism, one in which the psychological changes undergone by the patient mirror corresponding changes occurring in the therapist. Grace, under my care, drew upon our bond to assemble a newly-coherent sense of her own personal identity, even as I, under the guidance of Austin Des Lauriers, brought all that I was learning from him into an integrated psychotherapeutic orientation. In both of us, this process of personal transformation included a coming to terms with catastrophic loss and an awakening of deep mourning.

3

CREDO—PHENOMENOLOGICAL EXPLORATIONS AND REFLECTIONS

George E. Atwood

What follows are some reflections on my experiences as a psychotherapist, and also on the personal philosophy to which these experiences have led. The material is organized into a series of thought-trains centering on my work in the area of severe psychological disturbances.

1. Studying madness

As a young man, having just discovered the world of psychoanalysis, it occurred to me that the study of very severe psychological disturbances might lead to an understanding of the foundational constituents of human nature. Nothing could be more interesting, I thought, than to search for a new and deeper knowledge of the human condition as a psychotherapist. I have had the good fortune to pursue this quest for half a century.

One may ask the question: *what really is madness?* Here is how I would sum it up. Madness is not an illness or disease, it is not a condition existing somehow inside a person, and it is not a thing of any kind having objective existence. Madness is an experience a person may have, one involving at its essential core a fall into nonbeing. Madness is the dissolution of all order and a descent into chaos. It is the greatest catastrophe of subjectivity that can happen to a person. The felt reality of the world disintegrates and the enduring solidity and integrity of one's sense of selfhood—the ongoing experience of "I am"—becomes tenuous, unstable, and even vanishes. Madness is the abyss, and there is nothing more frightening, not even death.

Our minds can generate meanings and images of our deaths: we can picture the world surviving us, and we can identify with those that come later or otherwise try to immortalize ourselves through our works. We can rage against the dying of the light, and we can look forward to reunions with lost loved ones in the afterworld. We can think about the meaninglessness of human existence and its finitude. We can be relieved that all our sorrows will soon be over. We can even admire ourselves for being the only creatures in existence, as far as we know, who perceive their own wretched destiny to be extinguished. The abyss of madness offers no such possibilities—it is the end of all possible responses and meanings, the erasure of a world in which there is anything coherent to respond to, the melting away of anyone to engage in a response. It is much scarier than death, and this is shown by the fact that people in annihilation fear—the terror of madness—so often commit suicide rather than allow themselves to be engulfed by it.

In working with madness as a psychotherapist, one draws close to a realm in which there are no orienting landmarks, no coherent purposes and desires that point to a meaningful future, no organized recollections establishing a continuous past. The ordering structures of existence itself collapse, all sense of personal identity becomes erased, and one may fear being pulled out of one's sanity and into the nothingness. This is the terror of madness, and it affects all those who come into its vicinity.

How can we, as explorers of the human soul, enter this dark territory? I think we need a map of that chaos, a picture of the variations we will encounter, and some general guidelines as to how we might respond to the disastrous human situations that are encountered. Also needed are protections from how we are ourselves perceived. A terrible toll may be taken on the clinician who may be viewed as a persecutor, as a god, or even as a persecuting god. An even greater injury may be inflicted on the patient, someone already in the deepest trouble who now faces being seen as insane.

Psychotherapy is a world within the world, one in which patient and therapist gaze into each other's eyes and see themselves reflected in ways that may clash profoundly with what they feel is true or most deeply need. The mismatching of such images leads to all manner of difficulties for both parties, often spiraling into chronic impasses and the loss of the possibility of a therapeutic connection.

How can we as therapists be shielded against the terror of being drawn into the madness and against the potential violence to ourselves of the interplay with those who are lost in chaos? What protections can there be that will not operate as well at the expense of the patient? The key lies in one thing only—the power of human understanding. We must understand annihilation states and all the signs and symptoms expressing a person's struggle with such experiences. We must know the symbols typically used to represent these states of mind, images that are often concretized or reified, i.e., treated as tangible, substantial realities. We must use our understanding then to discover responses to our patients' crises that will help them re-find a personal center and feel included again in the human community. This is the work of clinical psychotherapy research, a field now on the threshold of a new age as the older ideas about objectified "mental illnesses" recede and a new emphasis on phenomenology arises.

Let me offer a thought on systems of psychiatric diagnosis, which everyone who enters our field encounters. Sometimes these systems turn into dragons that consume the minds of those who use them. There is nothing wrong with careful studies of the symptoms and signs of psychological disturbances, or with efforts to classify the richly-varied phenomena one sees in this realm of study. Ordering principles need to be applied, so that we are not just left adrift in a sea of confusion. A problem arises, however, when the classifications we impose on the variations that are observed become reified and objectified, turned into *mental diseases* imagined as existing somehow inside the people we seek to understand. Our patients in extreme distress reify their fantasies, generally in order to substantiate personal realities that have come under assault and are threatened with dissolution. We in parallel often reify our diagnostic concepts, ascribing the chaotic manifestations confronting us to a disease process inside the patient. Such a locating of the problem in the internal, not grounded in any actual scientific knowledge, basically takes the clinician off the hook. He or she is not implicated in what is seen; instead, the clinician sits high and dry, observing and classifying from a position of serene detachment, wrapped in a *cordon sanitaire*. This shields us from feeling responsible for how we are experienced and utterly neutralizes the power of the patient's attributions to attack or displace our own ways of defining ourselves. The problem is that the clinician *is* implicated—what people show us depends in part on how we are responding to them. Human experience is always embedded in a relational context. If that response organizes itself around an objectifying psychiatric diagnosis, one can expect to see reactions to the distancing and invalidation that is involved. If those very reactions are then ascribed again to the supposed mental illness, the distancing is deepened and the disjunction rigidifies. It is important to learn about diagnostic systems, but we must not let them become our commanding, reifying viewpoints. One should be guided instead by attention to the patients' experiences and by reflections on one's own. We are still at the beginning of exploring this strange and complicated country.

2. Secrets of the mind

In my youthful enthusiasm long ago, I imagined that a careful analysis of the fragments into which psychiatric patients disintegrate might disclose the basic elements of human nature. Although I have tried to follow through on this quest, I cannot say that I have succeeded in any literal sense. There is, however, one central discovery that has occurred as a result of this journey—myself. Amidst the shattered hearts, the broken minds, the annihilations, it is as if the pattern of my own life was somehow inscribed. Exploring the souls of my patients therefore has led me again and again to the depths and origins of my own lifeworld. Could it be that the study of madness presents us all with opportunities to discover who we most deeply are? Could it also be that the effort to assist those who come to us presents us with a chance to ameliorate our own wounds as well?

I shall tell about one of my own early experiences in this connection. My first seriously challenging patient, a young woman I met decades ago and discussed in detail in the previous chapter, believed with all her heart that she was a part of the

Holy Trinity and that she was one with God. She and I, over the tumultuous course of our early relationship, came to an understanding of her situation as centrally relating to a catastrophe that had occurred in her childhood—the sudden suicide of her beloved father. I saw how the tragic loss had bisected her youth into before and after, into father and no father. As our shared journey continued and her emotional integration began, I became witness to a gradual smoothing-out of the traumatic bifurcation with the emergence of feelings of furious rage, of heartbreaking sorrow, of annihilating invalidation. At some point along the way—I cannot say precisely when—it dawned on me that in looking at her life I was also seeing an image of my own. You see, my childhood also was divided into a before and an after, the separation caused by the sudden death of my mother when I was a young boy. In coming to the tragedy that had disastrously affected my patient's development, I had been returned to the tragedy of my own. In witnessing her slow attainment of wholeness, in turn, my own mending—continuing down to the present day—had a chance to begin. The great German philosopher–historian Wilhelm Dilthey (1926) famously proclaimed that in the study of persons in the so-called human sciences, all understanding is a matter of "the rediscovery of the I in the Thou." It follows from this elegant idea, to my mind anyway, that in the discovery of the Thou, we find a mirror in which our own souls are made visible.

Here are some additional thoughts that come forward as I think about the goal of finding out the secrets of human nature from the study of madness. I shall introduce them by describing the adventures of a young man I knew many years ago. He came to me just before a long psychiatric hospitalization. He said he had discovered the secret, not of human nature, but of the universe as a whole—the key to all of creation. I asked him to tell me about this amazing secret. He said it was revealed to him in a vision in which he saw the interrelatedness of all things. The vision encompassed the whole of the cosmos in a single image, abolishing all separateness and isolation in an overpowering, radiant unity. He had discovered the heart and soul of existence itself, and repeatedly shouted the secret out—"ALL IS ONE, ALL IS ONE, ALL IS ONE!"

I was curious about the personal context of this unifying vision. His life story was a sad one, involving a world in which the center failed to hold. He had been a golden child, a precocious genius who from an early age had shown stunning abilities in both science and the arts. His parents considered him to be a gift from God, filling their otherwise rather empty lives with a transcendent meaning. Complying with their expectations, the boy grew up with A-plus achievements in every endeavor, and the parents believed they had brought a great man into the world. The breakdown occurred on the eve of his graduation from college, a summa cum laude on the threshold of glorious success in life. One little problem tripped him up—a girlfriend he had become very attached to decided to end their relationship. His love for her, such as it was, expressed a part of him that contained, tenuously, his personal truth. Being a stellar achiever had always come easy and fit perfectly into his parents' needs. Losing the girlfriend was different; it was a disaster beyond imagining for a boy who had so little he could call truly his own. It was the end of a life that had scarcely begun. Unspeakable agonies followed the loss, a suffering beyond all comprehension in which everything that had seemed together was now torn asunder.

This was when the vision of cosmic oneness supervened. Every atom and subatomic particle, and every galaxy supercluster came together before him, in a vast network of interdependent relations. It was a breathtakingly beautiful tapestry encompassing the totality of all existing things. People in this young man's social world—family, friends, college teachers—thought he had gone crazy, and the decision was made to hospitalize him. What he was doing, however, was putting the world back together again, reconnecting all that had fallen apart.

I came to the idea that his vision was utterly, profoundly a true one. He had indeed encountered a secret of the universe, one that has been thoroughly hidden from us in this age of atomism. We think of our own lives as a matter of isolated minds existing alongside each other, little separate unit-selves dropped into the world out of their mothers' wombs. We imagine our minds as having interiors, filled with all manner of mental contents (thoughts, desires, memories, etc.), but subsisting somehow separately from a surrounding external environment. The estrangement between internal and external is paralleled by a dualism between our bodies and our minds. The universe itself, in turn, we visualize as a vast space populated by all things great and small, some of them causally interacting with one another but each of them having its own separate and solitary existence. We are hypnotized by this alienating and fragmenting atomism, regarding it as just the way things are rather than as the interpretive ontology that it is. My young man, propelled by a catastrophic experience of the disintegration of the world, broke through the trance of this philosophy to a sudden recognition of the unity of all beings. I found his thinking to be powerful, although at the time I met him he was unable to do much with it other than to cry and shout.

Working with those who dwell in the extreme range of psychological disorder presents us with dramatic signs of how our very selfhood and sense of the reality of the world are embedded in contexts shared with other human beings. One sees, for example, how the "symptoms" of so-called mental illness do not emanate from a wholly internal condition afflicting the isolated individual, but instead vary as a function of the response that person encounters from others. When responses felt as objectification and invalidation are supplanted by experiences of being understood and included in the community of others, striking shifts occur in delusions and hallucinations, and chronic annihilation states recede. C.G. Jung, the great psychiatrist, acknowledged this in his famous words: "Schizophrenics cease to be schizophrenic at the moment they feel understood" (Laing, 1959). We, as clinicians, are therefore involved in the psychological disturbances we are called upon to treat, and the wounds requiring our understanding in our patients are matched by the wounds we carry in our own hearts.

But there is more. The universe exists in such a way as to generate the possibility of our own coming into being, and a profound argument can be made that it is as it is in part because we are here to be aware of it. Human beings are implicated in the way in which the world becomes manifest, and at the same time the study of the cosmos is the universe becoming conscious of itself. The observer and the observed, in both the natural sciences and the human sciences, are inseparable from each other, and the constituents of reality, on smaller and smaller scales, turn out to be interdependent, entangled phenomena rather than fully separable units somehow subsisting in ontological solitude.

In other words, my young man was absolutely right. One might wonder what happened to him. It is sad. He was diagnosed on the basis of the grandiose euphoria he showed—*manic-depressive illness* was the diagnosis. The treatment provided to him included multiple hospitalizations, extensive electroconvulsive therapy, and an ever-varying succession of antipsychotic drugs. The last time I saw him, 15 years into this so-called treatment, he was doing poorly—depressed, confused, unable to work, obese, and . . . no girlfriend. I wonder what the outcome might have been if someone instead had been able to sit down with him—for a day, or a year, or a decade—and discuss what it meant that all is one. Is it not possible that good things might have emerged from such conversations?

A final thought regarding the story I have been telling: how is it that this young man, in captivity to his parents but also in a struggle to render a shattered universe whole, was a mirror in which I could find a reflection of myself? When I was a young college student, I made a discovery of my own that was very similar. In the context of an exposure to Zen Buddhism, it came to me that all dualism is false—every one of the great contrasts in our culture's history and philosophy —internal/external, matter/spirit, masculine/feminine, good/evil, freedom/ determinism, I/You—was illusory, and our belief in them was a trance from which we needed to awaken. Looking back, I see the philosophy of monistic adualism I then adopted as importantly related to the shattering trauma of my mother's death. I also see it as a precursor to the unifying theories and philosophical ideas in which I have come to believe.

3. Joy and suffering

The intensive psychotherapy of severe mental illness, so-called, offers two intertwining opportunities. On the one hand, one has a chance to give help to a fellow human being who is in trouble, perhaps the deepest psychological trouble that there is; on the other hand, one encounters phenomena that are at the far extreme of human experience, showing fundamental issues of all our lives with extravagant clarity and drama. This is the heart and soul of psychoanalysis, ever since it first appeared in the thinking of Sigmund Freud. Psychoanalysis is and always has been an approach to the healing of the wounded soul, and also an exploring of the depths of human existence and human nature. At the age of 17, I saw these twin pathways of the psychoanalytic enterprise, and I could not hold back from making a total commitment to the work. Is there anything that could possibly be as interesting or important?

There are great rewards to be found in working clinically in the realm of madness, but often enough there can also be great suffering. To engage with people in the extremes of psychological disorder is to cast oneself into the chaos—it means to embark upon a journey without an outcome that is certain, often with harrowing developments along the way, always requiring a commitment that is absolute. Sometimes, this journey eventuates in a mending and a thriving; in other instances, all our efforts may fail and we are consigned then to bear witness to someone's devastation. Therein lies the suffering, in the knowledge that nothing is assured and that catastrophe is always at hand. On the other side, our commitment, being absolute, means there also is hope for amelioration and emotional integration, and there is something utterly wonderful about pursuing this hope with nothing held back. If things do not work out, and perhaps there is a suicide or some other incontrovertible disaster, we die a thousand deaths. If, on the other hand, a better way is found, the phoenix rises from the ashes, and one then has the sense of having participated in the sacred.

During my college years I had a professor who repeatedly warned his students away from pursuing individual psychotherapy as a career. "How many people can you hope to help in a lifetime," he asked, "25 or 30 as a maximum, right?" It was his idea that our field should devote itself to the prevention of psychological disorders, through various social engineering programs based on behaviorist principles of reinforcement. I found his thoughts bleak and very depressing, because he was attacking the dream that brought me into psychology in the first place. I was too young to be able to offer much of a coherent response, but I knew I disliked what he was saying intensely. I now think that individual psychotherapy is itself the single most powerful preventive measure one could possibly find, because it has become apparent to me that giving help to one person can save the whole world. Psychological disturbances arise out of personal histories of traumatic experience, histories that are in turn embedded in complex intergenerational cycles. Traumas that remain unprocessed, that perhaps are not even recognized as having happened, are inevitably passed on to the next generation, and the next; and so it goes, as chains of historical causation reach across the years and even the decades and the centuries.

Consider the potential then that lies within even a single instance of individual psychotherapy that works out well, as the incomparable power of human understanding is brought to bear on a life that otherwise might have unfolded as just another destructive link in the historical sequence. The chain is broken, and, rather than darkness being delivered down upon one's descendants, an illumination is bequeathed as the effects of therapeutic transformation are transmitted instead. What my teacher failed to take into account is that emotional integration is contagious, radiating into the human surround and having repercussions that flow indefinitely into the future. How limited he was! And yet, we could ask what were *his* traumas, and why did he imagine he could fix them by his vast program of behaviorist engineering? As I reflect upon these questions, a picture of his unacknowledged despair comes into view. Behaviorism was like that—an intellectual movement turning toward the purely physical but predicated ultimately on the loss of hope for human connection.

There is also the intellectual joy that comes with understanding a life. I will give a single example. This is about the famous actress, Patty Duke, a person whose experiences interested me some years ago. Picture the following: as a young woman, she set off on a mission to rescue America from foreign influences, which she believed had infiltrated the highest offices of our government. A disastrous effort to travel to the White House in Washington, DC and personally eject the imaginary foreign agents was followed up by a devastating depression. In studying Duke's delusional mission and its background in her life history, I discovered that her earliest years were ones of enslavement to the entertainment industry: her parents essentially surrendered her to television agents who made her a nationally-acclaimed star, but at the price of a stolen childhood. It seemed apparent that the intruders in the White House were symbols of the controlling agendas of the public entertainment world. An autobiography was eventually written, describing her development and her breakdowns (*A Brilliant Madness*, Duke and Hochman, 1992). This record of the journey of her soul, however, had a peculiar feature—half of the chapters, interposed between those that she herself authored, were written by a science journalist representing medical psychiatry and chronicle her evolution as a victim of a biologically-based mental disease (so-called manic-depressive illness). Her account thus oscillates between two positions—one being that of telling her story as she experienced it and in her own words, and the other involving her surrender to medical authority. The chapters written embodying the psychiatric viewpoint were like the invaders in the White House, whereas in her own chapters her soul shines forth in freedom—or tries to. The early history of her life being taken over by the agendas of others, the delusion about foreign infiltrators inserting themselves into our country's self-government, and the strange structure of the autobiography thus display a repeating thematic pattern, centering on a heartbreaking, often losing battle to establish the integrity and inviolability of her own unique selfhood. The disparate elements here interrelate and form a tapestry that is beautiful, in its sad order and symmetry.

Human lives are like that. They display an invariant thematic structure, once apprehended in sufficient depth. I am not saying all our worlds are organized around a battle for self-integrity, as in the story of Patty Duke; I am saying that our individual life histories leave unique signatures on our personal universes. My life exhibits such patterns, and so does everyone's. A sense of intense and sometimes thrilling satisfaction accompanies the recognition of these unifying themes, in oneself and in others, as initially disparate elements become woven together and apparent chaos gives way to crystallizing order. There is joy in the unveiling of such things. In extending the ideas on which these analyses draw to the larger field of human existence as a whole, we recognize that the themes of the individual lives we encounter belong to a network of possibilities shared by us all.

4. The future of our field

Our time is one of immense change and loss. We are witness to the progressive falling-away of traditional answers to the question of the ultimate, as the solid foundations that once gave our lives meaning disappear in a whirlwind of available facts and diverse contexts and perspectives. Our time is also, though, one of great possibility. As the strictures of reassuring faith have dissolved, we have been cast into an open space, one that can only be filled in by our own creativity. Anxiety and uncertainty are inevitable companions in this journey, but so is the joy of anticipating what is to come. I want to imagine an emerging worldview that has been preparing itself for more than 100 years, and that is already having important consequences for our field. Three features seem to me salient in this new way of interpreting the meaning of human existence: interdependence, self-reflection, and responsibility.

1. A person is of his or her world, natural and social. The world that we experience is part of our very being, making us who and what we are. That constitutive world, at the same time, is what we make of it. A new mindset of radical interdependence is appearing, within which these statements do not stand in contradiction to each other.
2. Reflective awareness of the many contexts that shape our lives has in our time become pervasive, meaning that we are aware that all our beliefs and values—philosophical, religious, political, scientific—are embedded in our personal existence. One might say that the age of absolutes standing outside the circle of reflection is over. The yearning for ultimate answers and eternal foundations, however, seems likely to be a part of who we are forever.
3. Recognizing that all human beings are siblings in the same darkness (Stolorow, 2011), we are at last embracing the idea that we are our brothers' and sisters' keepers. We have also taken up the task of being guardians of the Earth and all its living creatures. I foresee a world in which these responsibilities are considered sacred. One might wonder how I can be so sanguine, in an age of terrorism and fanaticism. I regard these things as the death throes of religious ideologies that are giving way to a new humanism.

The theme of interdependence leads to a reconceptualization of what it means to be an individual person. One might say: there is no such *thing* as a person. I am obviously not claiming that people don't exist; it is rather that their existence is not one of being an isolated object, subsisting in a state of ontological separateness and solitude. The new worldview opens us to seeing our irreducible relatedness to our worlds and to others. This changes everything in how one understands so-called psychopathology. I will illustrate what I am saying with a clinical story.

A woman, 24 years old, was brought to a hospital by her father and mother after she had been arrested for trying to break into a well-known country musician's home. I happened to be on the clinical staff and so met this young person. She was mute, and scarcely moving. The word *catatonia* was used by two of our psychiatrists, engaging in diagnostic deliberations at the time, but I have never thought much of such labels. I sat quietly by her side on a daily basis in the first weeks of my work with her, hoping she would eventually begin to speak to me. Finally, she did, telling of a secret world in which she had lived for several years. This world was ruled by a famous country music star, and contained a number of other figures who regularly talked to her in the mornings and in the nights. They were like the chorus in a Greek tragedy. A love affair had developed between her and the star, conducted via telepathy, and she had been able for a long time to function in her world (she had been a part-time student in college) while dwelling much of the time in the secret realm.

Disaster came when she finally made an effort to have physical contact with her lover. The police had arrested her when she went to his actual home. The voices of the chorus, originally loving and sweet, had in the meantime turned increasingly critical and aggressive. Such idealized delusional companions often turn into persecutors, and the imaginary realm that has been found then becomes an unbearable hell. This patient was very similar to Joanne Greenberg (1964), who wrote a classic work in the literature of madness: *I Never Promised You a Rose Garden*. Joanne also inhabited a secret world, initially a place of magic and love but then turning dark and monstrous.

Traditional psychiatric thinking would understand this story as involving a dreadful mental illness that erupted in this woman's young life, an illness it calls schizophrenia. This was the diagnosis she was given during the period of her hospitalization. When looked upon within the new worldview, however, the symptoms of this so-called illness are no longer seen as emanating solely from a pathological condition somehow existing inside of her; instead, they are understood as having meaning within complex relational and historical contexts, as significantly relative to what had happened and was still happening in her social world.

Her emotional history, as I came to understand it in the long course of our contacts, centered on a theme of abiding loneliness. This context, unseen as such by members of her family of origin, was one in which she had accommodated herself to parental expectations and needs, becoming a child fulfilling their dreams through stellar academic achievements. The parents' marriage had at the same time been a bloody chaos of tension and hostility—repeatedly, the mother and the father had fought physically and threatened to abandon each other. She had tried, with all her might, to be a shining manifestation of hope for familial cohesion, always sensitive to her mother and father, moving back and forth between them, forever striving to make them proud and happy.

The extremity of this young girl's commitment to pleasing her parents and forestalling the disintegration of her family began at some point to lead to a division in her subjective life: on the one side were her harmonizing accommodations; on the other was an unarticulated and yet intensifying sense of hurt and of her own abandonment. There was no real recognition or validation of her pain by anyone, and therefore nowhere to go with her emerging suffering. This was the setting, following a series of separations and other changes in her living situation, in which she found her true love during her late teen years. Listening to his songs of loss and alienation, of broken hearts and searing loneliness, she saw her own experiences set to music; she had found a twin, a soulmate whose feelings precisely mirrored her own. Appearing recurrently in her dreams and reveries, his presence suddenly one day became utterly real, and she immersed herself in their shared affection, magically expressed through mental telepathy. Catastrophe occurred when she finally tried to establish physical contact with him.

I worked closely with her for many years, helping her to find words for her deep feelings of isolation and loneliness, and helping her as well to resist the siren-call of her lover and the chorus of voices associated with him. That is what is needed in such cases—patience, devotion, and understanding. I don't want to make it sound easy; it wasn't. There were a great many back and forth movements with respect to the secret world, and there were dangerous suicide attempts in the first years of our contacts. I suffered greatly with how close she came to ending her life. But it eventually worked out well enough. She brought herself together in gradual stages and found new ways to connect with others, expressing in her life a wonderful creative spirit.

I have told this little story to illustrate what I think will become commonplace in our field within the worldview I have been talking about. This young woman's psychological disturbance, her "schizophrenia," is here seen as a set of reactions embedded in her life in her family, and related to her trauma history and to the absence in her background of validating recognition. Her illness was not, from this standpoint, a pathology afflicting her entirely from within; it was a personal disaster brought on by complex transactional patterns inhering in her relationships over time to all those who were important to her, both real and imagined.

⋆ ⋆ ⋆

A great task facing us in the years ahead will be the thorough phenomenological re-description and reconceptualization of severe psychological disorders, and then a corresponding development of psychotherapeutic approaches embodying the new understandings that are attained. Great strides in this project have already occurred, and so we will not be starting from scratch. Among the many contributors on whose phenomenological and clinical contributions one can build, I would list: Jung, Tausk, Federn, Winnicott, Sullivan, Fromm-Reichman, Binswanger, Searles, Laing, Des Lauriers, Kohut, Karon, Stolorow, and Brandchaft.

Let me suggest some ideas that are more specific in regard to the most meaningful directions of our field in the coming decades. If I had another 30 years to live and to work, I might throw myself into the following sorts of things.

So-called schizophrenia

An influential book appeared in 1911—Eugen Bleuler's *Dementia Praecox or the Group of Schizophrenias*. In addition to introducing the term *schizophrenia* to our world, this work attempted to describe and provide examples of widely differing forms of the most extreme psychological disturbances that exist. It is worth reading even today for its rich accounts of madness in its many variations, although the work does suffer from some serious limitations from our present vantage point. The clinical descriptions are framed within a broadly Cartesian, intrapsychic frame of reference, locating the disturbances being considered inside the patients who are then pictured in isolation from their worlds. The presentations, in addition, tend to be restricted to the patients' symptomatology in the present moment, leaving out of account the complex histories and relational contexts in which their symptoms are embedded and have meaning. Finally, the book is written almost entirely from the perspective of the medical model, viewing psychological disturbances as disease processes occurring in the mind.

A very wonderful project, one that would require a great many years of devotion, would be the modern counterpart to Bleuler's classic study. This would involve even more detailed descriptions and examples of madness in its many forms and variations, with the focus however always being on the subjective states that are involved. Such a phenomenological emphasis would then be accompanied by a life-historical perspective, from which the overt symptom-pictures are cast in relation to the personal backgrounds of the people concerned. There would only be one way to accomplish the immense task I am suggesting—the collaboration of a number of dedicated clinicians and thinkers. It would be required that there be long-term commitments to the patients being studied, so that the inquiry into their worlds have a grounding in deep explorations of history and also include the nature of the therapeutic processes that can be achieved.

Bleuler proposed that the heart of what was known in his time as dementia praecox consisted in various splitting processes occurring in the mind; hence the term *schizo-phrenia*. These included the disintegration of the logical associations of thought, the splitting of cognition from its associated affects, the dividing of positive and negative emotions, and the separating off of a private reality from contact with the externally real. My own view is that future phenomenological studies of patients in this range will show how these various features can be significantly understood as secondary to a sense of personal annihilation. This means that the primary disturbance would be seen in the shattering or even erasure of the experience of personal selfhood. Also central would be the dissolution of the sense of the realness of the world and the disintegration of all that we ordinarily experience as substantial and enduring. The most prominent visible symptoms of these disturbances, such as one sees in hallucinations and delusions, in this context appear as restitutive or reparative reactions, efforts to reunify all that has fallen apart and re-solidify all that has melted away.

Another clinical story comes to mind that relates to the sort of understanding I am thinking of. Consider this brief account as standing for 100 that I could provide. One of my patients from many years ago came to me after a long period in a psychiatric hospital. 21 years old at the time, she described herself as having always been in "pieces," having separate and distinct "selves" that floated about in a strange space, without there being a common center. There was a sexual self, a religious self, a political self, a comical self, a professional self, and a social self. Each of these entities embodied an area of her interests and capabilities, but they were like islands suspended in the sea with no land bridges between them. It was interesting to me that a delusion haunting her during the many months of her hospitalization was a belief that she was part of a world-revolution aiming to dissolve traditional nation-states and establish a universal government based on the power of all-embracing love. Out of her own personal fragmentation, it seemed, was arising a dream of world unity. She had been told by her doctors her diagnosis was that of schizophrenia, and, confused about what this meant, studied Bleuler's derivation of the term from the Greek words for "split" and "mind." She told me that a better translation, still respecting the etymology but connecting more closely to her own familiar self-experience, would be *torn soul*. I found her statement, obviously rooted in her feeling of being in pieces, to be one of the most astute things I have ever heard on this subject, and I told her so. We worked together for several decades and got along very well.

So-called bipolar disorder

In *The Abyss of Madness* (Atwood, 2011), I made the claim that the most important frontier for present-day clinical psychoanalytic research is that of the psychotherapy of bipolar disorder, also known as manic-depressive illness. Of course, these terms are medical-diagnostic designations, embedded in a Cartesian, objectifying world-view. How the patients so diagnosed will appear under a phenomenological lens remains to be seen, and what innovations in our approach to them will come forth are still to be defined.

A fabulous insight into the experiential core of a great many of the patients showing an oscillating pattern of mania and depression was given to us by Bernard Brandchaft. In his book *Toward an Emancipatory Psychoanalysis* (Brandchaft, Doctors, and Sorter, 2010), he saw a problem again involving a sense of personal annihilation, wherein the manic episode expresses a transitory liberation from annihilating ties to caregivers. The depression that ensues, in contrast, represents the reinstatement of those ties. A division has occurred between accommodative and individualizing trends in these patients' personalities: on one side of this division, there is a compliant surrender to authority and the installation within the patient's selfhood of others' purposes and expectations; on the other side is a glorious overthrow of such captivity and the embrace of shining freedom. The magical emancipation, of course, cannot last, because there is nothing and no one to support it, and so it collapses into a dark despair. Here would be my questions for those who seek pathways of psychotherapy with such patients in the future: can an experience be facilitated that establishes a new center, one in which compliance and rebellion are somehow integrated? Can the empathy of the clinician become a medium in which previously aborted developmental processes can be reinstated? Can a deep understanding of what is at stake for the patient finally make a constructive difference to his or her destiny in the continuing nightmare of bipolarity?

The great psychoanalyst, Frieda Fromm-Reichman, in 1954 published a now-classic clinical study. Its title was: "An intensive study of twelve cases of manic-depressive psychosis." A generalization arising from this study was the notion that such patients were, in their families growing up, treated as extensions of their caregivers rather than as independent beings in their own rights. I would like to see a contemporary counterpart to this work, tracing carefully the subjective worlds and histories of bipolar patients and exploring the outer limits of our efficacy as therapists in arresting their destructive patterns and stabilizing their lives. The key to success in such a project will be in the new understanding flowing from Brandchaft's insight, one highlighting the patients' needs to find pathways of emancipation from enslaving accommodation that do not lead into the structureless chaos of the manic episode.

An amazing example of the twin-sides of bipolarity is given in another classic of the literature of madness—Kay Jamison's *An Unquiet Mind* (1995). This author tells the story of her extended resistance as a young woman against her doctor on the issue of her taking mood-stabilizing drugs. Back and forth their arguments went, with her trying to defend her right to a life free of medical intrusions, and with her psychiatrist telling her she had a biologically-based mental illness that absolutely required medications in order for her to be able to function. Finally, with the greatest reluctance, Kay agreed to begin on a course of taking regular doses of lithium. However, when she went to the pharmacy to pick up her prescription, she suddenly was seized by a terrifying vision. She saw, in her mind's eye, vast numbers of poisonous snakes approaching her vicinity and foresaw how these dangerous creatures would strike at her and all those she cared about, filling their bodies with lethal toxins. So, she purchased, along with her lithium, all the snakebite kits the pharmacy had available, hoping to use the kits to save herself and as many people as she could.

Here is my theory of what this delusion about snakes symbolized. The poison carried by these imagined creatures, about to be injected into Kay herself and the unsuspecting public, represented the diagnostic authority of her doctor, to which she was in the process of capitulating. The theme of at first fighting back wilfully but then caving in and surrendering appears also in her early family life, which she describes as having been a battle against oppressive control. The side of this woman tending toward compliant surrender was accepting into her self-definition the medical attributions she had earlier resisted; the side of her wanting to protect her self-integrity from invasion and usurpation armed itself with antidotes to snake venom. There is a parallel between Kay's desperate purchase of the life-saving snakebite kits and Patty Duke's attempt to drive imagined foreign agents out of the White House. Remarkably, neither of these women appears to have had any awareness of such symbolic connections. So-called bipolar patients often seem to live in a world of utter concreteness, rendering subjective life strangely opaque.

Madness and creative genius

Another favorite subject of mine, one that I hope will be taken up in our field in coming years, pertains to creativity and its complex relationships to madness and trauma. It is my view that the events and circumstances of our lives that hurt us most deeply, sometimes that even take us into an experience of personal annihilation, are implicated as also being among the factors leading to great achievements of creative imagination.

I taught an advanced seminar at my college for a long time, a class in which each year we would select a person for study showing great creativity but also signs of madness. A generalization unexpectedly emerged from the long series of analyses that took place: in almost every case, there was evidence of a profound, irreconcilable conflict in the personality of the creator, one that threatened to lead to fragmentation and madness but that seemed to be integrated by the acts of creation. The specific content of the division varied from instance to instance, but the presence of such a duality seemed not to. Four such divided geniuses are described and discussed in the final chapter of *The Abyss of Madness*: Søren Kierkegaard, Friedrich Nietzsche, Martin Heidegger, and Ludwig Wittgenstein.

I would be very interested in a much more inclusive exploring of major figures in art, philosophy, and science in order to see just how truly general this apparent pattern is. It would also be important to study carefully how it is that the creative activity brings the warring trends in the creator's soul into a unity. I am thinking that a thorough understanding of such matters could lead to innovative psychotherapeutic approaches with people otherwise fated to lives of paralysis and despair. Would it not be a beautiful development in our field if ways could be found to transform delusions and hallucinations into works of art?

I shall offer a single instance of the analyses conducted in my college seminar—that of the great German poet Rainer Maria Rilke. Rilke's writings abound with a concern with spirits and ghosts. He was himself inhabited by the soul of a sister who died, a short period before he was born. His mother, broken-hearted by her loss, raised her son to be the dead child's reincarnation. Consider his name, as it was given to him by his mother—René Karl Wilhelm Josef Maria Rilke. The name *Rainer*, which one normally associates with him, does not appear in this sequence. It is a masculinization of *René*, originally given as his first name. He changed it under the influence of his muse and lover, Lou Andreas Salome.

Rilke's given names form a sequence of male designations bounded at the beginning and the end by female ones. His mother, having lost her daughter, enclosed his name, and his soul, in a vision of a resurrected female. She dressed him in girls' clothes, encouraged his playing with dolls, and interpreted his early interests in drawing and watercolors as essentially feminine preoccupations. Born a boy, he was raised from birth to be a girl.

The soul of the dead sister took up residence inside the young boy. Although the female spirit never became the whole of him, she did alternate in his experience with the male child he also became. Sometimes, her presence was felt as a mystical mask he would put on; the problem arose when this mask began to melt into his face and displace his identity as a boy. Or was it the girl he was raised to be whose identity was displaced by the mask of a boy? At other times, the alien spirit erupted from within, draining away all vitality and pursuing its own independent agendas (Rilke, 1910). This spirit might have been, again, the girl emerging from within the boy, or the boy erupting from the depths of the girl his mother saw him as being. With Rilke, it is always both/and, and never either/or. The key to the genius of his poetry lies in his ability to embrace both sides of his androgynous nature, and this ability also shielded him from madness.

In the journey of the creator, there is almost always a division within the soul, one that—left unaddressed—carries the possibility of madness within its depths. The act of creation provides a pathway in which the division can be transcended and unified, and is a protection against psychological destruction. There are countless examples one can find in the life histories of artists, philosophers, and scientists. The need to bring together that which has been torn asunder establishes an everlasting tension, one that leads to a spiraling of creativity. This is a theme one could spend a lifetime studying.

5. The lost childhood of the therapist

There is a traumatic condition that has developed early in the lives of almost every psychotherapist I have known, or at least in the lives of those who become committed to working with very serious disorders. I will call this *the situation of the lost childhood*. There are two basic pathways along which it seems to occur.

The first and most frequent story is one in which a child is enlisted at a young age to support and sustain a depressed or otherwise emotionally-troubled parent. I am speaking here of something extreme, wherein a reversal of roles takes place and the parent comes to depend on the child rather than the other way around. The identity of the son or daughter then crystallizes around making nurturing provisions, the activity of caregiving being the only way open to maintaining bonds of secure connection in the family. There has generally been an emotional void in the parent's own background, and the child is then given the task of filling it. A compromise of the child's autonomy and authenticity occurs as the little "psychotherapist" materializes, a slave to the needs of the mother and/or father. Impulses to disengage and pursue a separate life in this context are felt by the parent as unbearable injuries, always producing reactions of great distress and sometimes of rage. When the child tries in some way to be a person in his or her own right, the parental response may be: "Why are you killing me?" This is a pathway closely resembling the one described by Alice Miller (1982) in her very fine book, *The Drama of the Gifted Child*. The "gift" to which she was referring here is the natural sensitivity and empathy of certain children that lead a wounded parent to draw them into this role. Miller's original title for her book was *Prisoners of Childhood*, a very apt description of the imprisoning effect of such an upbringing, which includes the dissociation of important sectors of the child's personality as the child is not allowed to become the person he or she might otherwise have been. The most natural thing in the world for such an individual, later grown up, is to seek out a career in counseling and psychotherapy. Their training for the work has been occurring from an early age. Thus is generated what I call a *Type 1 Clinician*, one seen especially frequently in the field of psychoanalysis.

The second situation leading to this career is based not on serving the needs of a troubled parent, but rather on an experience of traumatic loss. Here too there is an imprisonment that takes place, and a resultant lost childhood that compromises the full development of the individual's own unique personality.

The story runs as follows. A fundamentally loving relationship with one or both parents is in place in early life, a bond within which the emerging identity of the developing child is supported and the stability of family life is felt to be secure. An irrevocable change then occurs, something making it seem that formerly secure ties are lost, leaving the child bereft. A parent may grow ill and die, vanish for reasons unknown, be perceived as having disappointed or betrayed the child unforgivably, or undergo an emotional breakdown from which there is no recovery. The early world, now missing, becomes idealized in memory, contrasting sharply and painfully with the desolation that has taken its place. The longing for the parent who has inexplicably changed or disappeared intensifies and becomes unbearable. The loss of the mother or father at this point is restituted by an identification process, one in which the child *becomes* the one who has gone missing. A transformation of personal identity has thus taken place, in which the loving, rescuing qualities of the longed-for parental figure now reappear as aspects of the child's own selfhood. By the magical act of turning oneself into the absent beloved one, the trauma of loss is undone and the shattered, chaotic world is set right. In this way, a loving parental attitude is installed within the child's personality, and his or her subsequent relationships in every sphere of life come to be dominated by a theme of caregiving. Any breakdown of the identification with the idealized figure leads to a resurgence of the chaos and pain of the original loss.

This too can eventuate in a most terrible captivity, for the trajectory of the child's own development here has been interrupted and frozen by the need to stand in for the parent who has been lost. Who that child might have been or wanted to become as a distinctive person is thereby sidelined as the identification solidifies. One can appreciate how easy it would be for such a person to fall into a career as a psychotherapist. This is the situation of a *Type 2 Clinician*.

There would also be mixed cases, in which the early developmental history of the psychotherapist included both kinds of experiences, traumatic emotional exploitation by a disturbed parent *and* traumatic loss. I am myself an example of the second type, with the central loss being that of my mother when I was a boy. The great theorist D.W. Winnicott, if I have understood him correctly, was a clinician of the first type, affected most importantly by a mother who suffered from severe depressions. Obviously, there may be other pathways to choosing a life of service to the emotionally disturbed, but almost all of the clinicians I have known fall into one or both of my categories. My friend and colleague, Robert

Stolorow, on hearing about these ideas, suggested that he is himself "a mild case of Type 1." At first, I agreed with this notion, although I wasn't so sure about the supposed mildness. On further reflection I came to think he is a mixed case, with an early pattern of caregiving to wounded parents intertwined with issues of emotional desertion and loss that were magnified by devastating tragedy in his adult years (see Atwood and Stolorow, 2014, Chapter 7).

It runs through my mind that the great German philosopher Friedrich Nietzsche exemplifies the life theme I have called Type 2. He lost his beloved father at the age of 4, and reacted to the death by becoming his father once more; in the process, however, the child he had been disappeared as an active presence in his life. That is the downfall of this solution to loss: identifying with and thereby substituting for the missing parent leads to the disincarnation of the original child, whose independent hopes and dreams never have a chance to crystallize or be pursued. Nietzsche, catapulted at a young age into a precocious paternal maturity, became a psychotherapist for civilization itself, a kind of father figure (Zarathustra) for all humanity in its journey into an uncertain future. His prodigious creativity spiraled forth from the tensions generated by his personal tragedy, and so did his eventual madness.

The division between the two pathways I have described is not absolute and may be pictured too sharply. Those who are drawn into the role of soothing and healing a wounded parent are not strangers to the experience of disruptive separation and loss; correspondingly, those bereft children who identify with a lost mother or father are often doing so, in part, to repair a family that has been shattered by tragedy. Perhaps one could think of my Type 1 and Type 2 clinicians as opposite sides of the same coin, differing in individual lives only in their relative salience.

Anyone embarking on a career aiming to help people come to terms with their traumatic life situations and histories needs to do everything possible to address his or her own. In the early history of psychoanalysis, a requirement was established that analysts in training complete their own personal analyses before they could be officially certified. This seemed like a good idea at the time, decreed by Freud and Jung. These fathers of our field, however, exempted themselves from this requirement, which I think should upset analysts tremendously! Here is the problem. The analyst's unprocessed trauma, like the parent's, is inevitably passed on to the next generation. Freud and Jung, by refraining from applying their injunction to themselves, guaranteed that specific areas of their unconscious lives—those pertaining to their unattended wounds—would be visited upon their descendants. This is why our field's continuing interest in the lives of its progenitors is so important. Identifying zones of incompleteness in their self-analyses holds out the possibility of our emancipation from all they were unable to understand.

Clinicians must be aware of what has happened in their lives and grieve the losses they have incurred. Nothing else will do. The emotional integration of the traumas of which I am speaking is a lifetime project, and so the important thing is that the journey commences. Mourning needs to occur, both for the parent who was lost or was never there in the first place, and also for the unobstructed childhood that never had a chance to unfold. The psychotherapist's unification will be a theme in all of his or her work, most often in the background, but included nevertheless in any constructive developments that take place. Psychotherapy is not a procedure performed upon one person by another; it is a dialogue between personal universes, and it transforms both. Our field has not yet caught up to this idea, but the time is coming in which it will be regarded as axiomatic.

4

CREDO—INTERSUBJECTIVE-SYSTEMS THEORY

A phenomenological-contextualist perspective

Robert D. Stolorow

Intersubjective-systems theory, the name of my collaborators' and my (Stolorow, Atwood, and Orange, 2002) post-Cartesian psychoanalytic perspective, is a *phenomenological contextualism*. It is phenomenological in that it investigates and illuminates worlds of emotional experience. It is contextual in that it holds that such organizations of emotional experience take form, both developmentally and in the psychoanalytic situation, in constitutive intersubjective contexts.

Developmentally, recurring patterns of intersubjective transaction within the developmental system give rise to principles (thematic patterns, meaning-structures) that unconsciously organize subsequent emotional and relational experiences. Such organizing principles are unconscious, not in the sense of being repressed but in being prereflective: they ordinarily do not enter the domain of reflective self-awareness. These intersubjectively derived, prereflective organizing principles are the basic building blocks of personality development, and their totality constitutes one's character. They show up in the psychoanalytic situation in the form of transference, which intersubjective-systems theory conceptualizes as unconscious organizing activity. The patient's transference experience is co-constituted by the patient's prereflective organizing principles and whatever is coming from the analyst that is lending itself to being organized by them. A parallel statement can be made about the analyst's transference. The psychological field formed by the interplay of the patient's transference and the analyst's transference is an example of what we call an *intersubjective system*. Psychoanalysis is a dialogical method for bringing this prereflective organizing activity into reflective self-awareness.

Freud's psychoanalysis expanded the Cartesian mind, Descartes's (1641) "thinking thing," to include a vast unconscious realm. Nonetheless, the Freudian mind remained a Cartesian mind, a self-enclosed, worldless subject or mental apparatus containing and working over mental contents and ontologically separated from its surround. Corresponding to its Cartesianism is traditional psychoanalysis's objectivist epistemology. One isolated mind, the analyst, is claimed to make objective observations and interpretations of another isolated mind, the patient.

A phenomenological contextualism concerns emotional experience and its organization, not reified mind-entities, and, following Heidegger (1927), it reunites the Cartesian isolated mind with its world, its context. Correspondingly, intersubjective-systems theory embraces a perspectivalist epistemology, insisting that analytic understanding is always from a perspective shaped by the organizing principles of the inquirer. Accordingly, there are no objective or neutral analysts, no immaculate perceptions (Nietzsche, 1892), no God's-eye view (Putnam, 1990) of anyone or anything.

I hope it is already clear to the reader that our phenomenological emphasis does not in any way entail abandonment of the exploration of unconsciousness. Going back to the father of philosophical phenomenology, Edmund Husserl (1900, 1913), phenomenological inquiry has never been restricted to mere description of conscious experiences. Phenomenological investigation has always been centrally concerned with the structures that prereflectively organize conscious experience. Whereas philosophical phenomenologists are concerned with those structures that operate universally, a psychoanalytic phenomenologist seeks to illuminate those principles that unconsciously organize individual worlds of experience and, in particular, those that give meaning to emotional and relational experiences. Such principles include, importantly, those that dictate what emotional experiences must be prevented from coming into full being—that is, those that must be dynamically repressed—because they are prohibited or too dangerous. Intersubjective-systems theory emphasizes that all such forms of unconsciousness are constituted in relational contexts. Indeed, from an intersubjective-systems perspective, all of the clinical phenomena with which psychoanalysis has been traditionally concerned are seen as taking form within systems of interacting, differently organized, mutually influencing emotional worlds. Phenomenology led us inexorably to contextualism.

From mind to world: Intersubjectivity

Our first explicit use of the term *intersubjective* appeared in an article (Stolorow, Atwood, and Ross, 1978) that Lewis Aron (1996) credited with having introduced the concept of intersubjectivity into American psychoanalytic discourse. There, we conceptualized the interplay between transference and countertransference in psychoanalytic treatment as an intersubjective process reflecting the mutual interaction between the differently organized subjective worlds of patient and analyst, and we examined the impact on the therapeutic process of unrecognized correspondences and disparities—intersubjective conjunctions and disjunctions—between the patient's and analyst's respective worlds of experience. Eventually, we extended our intersubjective perspective to a wide array of clinical phenomena, including development and pathogenesis, transference and resistance, emotional conflict formation, dreams, enactments, neurotic symptoms, and psychotic states

(Stolorow, Brandchaft, and Atwood, 1987). In each instance, phenomena that had traditionally been the focus of psychoanalytic investigation were understood not as products of isolated intrapsychic mechanisms but as forming at the interface of interacting experiential worlds. The intersubjective context, we contended, plays a constitutive role in all forms of psychopathology, and clinical phenomena cannot be comprehended psychoanalytically apart from the intersubjective field in which they crystallize.

From drive to affectivity: Emotional trauma

It is a central tenet of intersubjective-systems theory that a shift in psychoanalytic thinking from the motivational primacy of drive to the motivational primacy of affectivity moves psychoanalysis toward a phenomenological contextualism and a central focus on dynamic intersubjective systems. Unlike drives, which are claimed to originate deep within the interior of a Cartesian isolated mind, affect—that is, subjective emotional experience—is something that from birth onward is co-constituted within ongoing relational systems. Emotional experience is inseparable from the intersubjective contexts of attunement and malattunement in which it is felt. Therefore, locating affect at its motivational center automatically entails a radical contextualization of virtually all aspects of human psychological life. This claim is nowhere more vividly exemplified than in the understanding of emotional trauma.

From an intersubjective-systems perspective, developmental trauma is viewed not as an instinctual flooding of an ill-equipped Cartesian container, as Freud (1926) would have it, but as an experience of unbearable affect. Furthermore, the intolerability of an affect state cannot be explained solely, or even primarily, on the basis of the quantity or intensity of the painful feelings evoked by an injurious event. Traumatic affect states can be grasped only in terms of the relational systems in which they are felt (Stolorow and Atwood, 1992, Chapter 4). Developmental trauma originates within a formative intersubjective context whose central feature is malattunement to painful affect—a breakdown of the child–caregiver inter-affective system, leading to the child's loss of affect-integrating capacity and thereby to an unbearable, overwhelmed, disorganized state. Painful or frightening affect becomes traumatic when the attunement that the child needs to assist in its tolerance and integration is profoundly absent.

From the claim that trauma is constituted in an intersubjective context wherein severe emotional pain cannot find a relational home in which it can be held, it follows that injurious childhood experiences in and of themselves need not be traumatic (or at least not lastingly so) or pathogenic, provided that they occur within a responsive milieu. *Pain is not pathology*. It is the absence of adequate attunement to the child's painful emotional reactions that renders them unendurable and thus a source of traumatic states and psychopathology. This conceptualization holds both for discrete, dramatic traumatic events and the more subtle "cumulative traumas" (Khan, 1963) that occur continually throughout childhood.

One consequence of developmental trauma, relationally conceived, is that affect states take on enduring, crushing meanings. From recurring experiences of malattunement, the child acquires the unconscious conviction that unmet developmental yearnings and reactive painful feeling states are manifestations of a loathsome defect or of an inherent inner badness. A defensive self-ideal is often established, representing a self-image purified of the offending affect states that were perceived to be unwelcome or damaging to caregivers. Living up to this affectively purified ideal becomes a central requirement for maintaining harmonious ties to others and for upholding self-esteem. Thereafter, the emergence of prohibited affect is experienced as a failure to embody the required ideal, an exposure of the underlying essential defectiveness or badness, and is accompanied by feelings of isolation, shame, and self-loathing. In the psychoanalytic situation, qualities or activities of the analyst that lend themselves to being interpreted according to such unconscious meanings of affect confirm the patient's expectations in the transference that emerging feeling states will be met with disgust, disdain, disinterest, alarm, hostility, withdrawal, exploitation, and the like, or will damage the analyst and destroy the therapeutic bond. Such transference expectations, unwittingly confirmed by the analyst, are a powerful source of resistance to the experience and articulation of affect. Intractable repetitive transferences and resistances can be grasped, from this perspective, as rigidly stable "attractor states" (Thelen and Smith, 1994) of the patient–analyst system, in which the meanings of the analyst's stance have become tightly coordinated with the patient's grim expectations and fears, thereby exposing the patient repeatedly to threats of retraumatization. The focus on affect and its meanings contextualizes both transference and resistance.

A second consequence of developmental trauma is a severe constriction and narrowing of the horizons of emotional experiencing (Stolorow, Atwood, and Orange, 2002, Chapter 3), so as to exclude whatever feels unacceptable, intolerable, or too dangerous in particular intersubjective contexts. When a child's emotional experiences are consistently not responded to or are actively rejected, the child perceives that aspects of his or her affective life are intolerable to the caregiver. These regions of the child's emotional world must then be sacrificed in order to safeguard the needed tie. Repression is grasped here as a kind of negative organizing principle, always embedded in ongoing intersubjective contexts, determining which configurations of affective experience are not to be allowed to come into full being. For example, when the act of linguistically articulating an affective experience is perceived to threaten an indispensable tie, repression can be achieved by preventing the continuation of the process of encoding that experience in language. In such instances, repression keeps affect nameless.

The focus on affect thus contextualizes the very boundary between conscious and unconscious. Unlike the Freudian repression barrier, viewed as a fixed intrapsychic structure within an isolated Cartesian container, the limiting horizons of emotional experiencing are conceptualized here as emergent properties of ongoing dynamic intersubjective systems. Forming and evolving within a nexus of living systems, the horizons of experiencing are grasped as fluid and ever-shifting, products both of the person's unique intersubjective history and of what is or is not allowed to be felt within the intersubjective fields that constitute his or her current living.

Like constricted and narrowed horizons of emotional experiencing, expanding horizons too can only be grasped in terms of the intersubjective contexts within which they take form. This claim holds important implications for conceptualizing the therapeutic action of psychoanalytic interpretation.

I have long contended that a good (i.e., a mutative) interpretation is a relational process, a central constituent of which is the patient's experience of having his or her feelings understood. Furthermore, it is the specific transference meaning of the experience of being understood that supplies its mutative power, as the patient weaves that experience into the tapestry of developmental longings mobilized by the analytic engagement. Interpretation does not stand apart from the emotional relationship between patient and analyst; it is an inseparable and, to my mind, crucial dimension *of* that relationship. In the language of intersubjective-systems theory, interpretive expansion of the patient's capacity for reflective awareness of old, repetitive organizing principles occurs concomitantly with the affective impact and meanings of ongoing relational experiences with the analyst, and both are indissoluble components of a unitary therapeutic process that establishes the possibility of alternative principles for organizing experience, whereby the patient's emotional horizons can become widened, enriched, more flexible, and more complex. As the tight grip of old organizing principles becomes loosened, as emotional experiencing thereby expands and becomes increasingly nameable within a context of human understanding, and as what one feels becomes seamlessly woven into the fabric of whom one essentially is, there is an enhancement of one's very sense of being. That, to my mind, is the essence of therapeutic change.

Returning to the theme of emotional trauma, I have found a phenomenological-contextualist perspective to be invaluable in illuminating not only trauma's context-embeddedness but also its existential significance. The key that, for me, unlocked the existential meaning of emotional trauma was what I came to call *the absolutisms of everyday life*:

> When a person says to a friend, "I'll see you later" or a parent says to a child at bedtime, "I'll see you in the morning," these are statements whose validity is not open for discussion. Such absolutisms are the basis for a kind of naïve realism and optimism that allow one to function in the world, experienced as stable and predictable. It is in the essence of emotional trauma that it shatters these absolutisms, a catastrophic loss of innocence that permanently alters one's sense of being-in-the-world. Massive deconstruction of the absolutisms of everyday life exposes the inescapable contingency of existence on a universe that is random and unpredictable and in which no safety or continuity of being can be assured. Trauma thereby exposes "the unbearable embeddedness of Being". . . . As a result, the traumatized person cannot

> help but perceive aspects of existence that lie well outside the absolutized horizons of normal everydayness. It is in this sense that the worlds of traumatized persons are fundamentally incommensurable with those of others, the deep chasm in which an anguished sense of estrangement and solitude takes form.
>
> (Stolorow, 2007, p. 16)

In shattering the tranquilizing absolutisms of everyday life, emotional trauma plunges us into a form of what Heidegger (1927) calls authentic (owned) Being-toward-death, wherein death and loss are apprehended as distinctive possibilities that are constitutive of our very existence, of our intelligibility to ourselves in our futurity and finitude—possibilities that are both certain and indefinite as to their "when" and that therefore always impend as constant threats. Stripped of its sheltering illusions, the everyday world loses its significance, and the traumatized person feels anxious and uncanny, no longer safely at home in the everyday world.

I have claimed that "trauma recovery" is an oxymoron—human finitude with its traumatizing impact is not an illness from which one can or should recover (Stolorow, 2011, Chapter 5). "Recovery" is a misnomer for the constitution of an expanded emotional world that coexists alongside the absence of the one that has been shattered by trauma. The expanded world and the absent shattered world may be more or less integrated or dissociated, depending on the degree to which the unbearable emotional pain evoked by the traumatic shattering has become integrated or remains dissociated defensively, which depends in turn on the extent to which such pain found a relational home, a context of human understanding, in which it could be held.

What makes the finding of such an understanding context possible? An answer to this question can be found in a relational dimension of the experience of finitude itself. Just as finitude is fundamental to our existential constitution, so too is it constitutive of our existence that we meet each other as siblings in the same darkness, deeply connected with one another in virtue of our *common* finitude (Stolorow, 2007, 2011). Thus, although the possibility of emotional trauma is ever present, so too is the possibility of forming bonds of deep emotional understanding within which devastating emotional pain can be held, rendered more tolerable, and eventually integrated. Our existential kinship-in-the-same-darkness is the condition for the possibility both of the profound contextuality of emotional trauma and of the mutative power of human understanding.

The implication of the foregoing formulations is that the proper therapeutic comportment toward another's emotional trauma may be characterized as a kind of emotional *dwelling*. We must not turn away from another's experience of trauma by offering false reassurances about time healing all wounds or empty platitudes about letting go and moving on. We offer such reassurances and platitudes when another's traumatized state confronts us with our own finitude and existential vulnerability, and so we turn evasively away. If we are to be an understanding relational home for a traumatized person, we must tolerate our own existential vulnerabilities so that we can dwell unflinchingly with his or her unbearable and recurring emotional pain. When we dwell with others' unendurable pain, their shattered emotional worlds are enabled to shine with a kind of sacredness that calls forth an understanding and caring engagement within which traumatized states can be gradually transformed into bearable painful feelings. Emotional pain and existential vulnerability that find a hospitable relational home can be seamlessly and constitutively integrated into whom one experiences oneself as being.

Dialogue

RDS: Comparing Chapters 3 and 4 (our "Credo" articles), it seems that your contributions to our phenomenological contextualism importantly arose out of the clinical context of the study and therapy of extreme (psychotic) states, whereas mine was powerfully influenced by the encounter between my own experience of a traumatic loss and Heidegger's existential philosophy. My chapter formalizes much of what you discovered in your early work.

In the book *Working Intersubjectively* (Orange, Atwood, and Stolorow, 1997), you contributed a chapter, "Contexts of nonbeing: Varieties of the experience of personal annihilation," which is a case in point. There, you offered a high-science chart of a number of dimensions on which the experience of self-loss can take place. This chart materializes a nascent conceptual scheme envisioned by the late Daphne Stolorow, whose untimely death prevented her from developing her thinking on this further. You/we have repeatedly emphasized that every significant alteration in self-experience is linked with a corresponding alteration in one's experience of the world as a whole. Can you develop this claim as it applies to the various dimensions of self-experience?

GEA: I think of the experience of one's selfhood as a central part of the organization of the subjective world. Any dramatic alteration in self-experience will accordingly have massive repercussions on the individual's world in general. How could it be otherwise? In my chapter in *Working Intersubjectively*, I broke the experience of self down into several dimensions—inner cohesion, temporal continuity, affectivity, agency, subjectivity, differentiation, psychosomatic unity—and I pictured various forms of personal annihilation as involving a self-loss experience on one or more of these dimensions. I suppose one could take annihilation experiences, dimension by dimension, and ask about the transformations of world-experience that correlate with them. For example, consider extreme self-loss on the dimension of temporal continuity, a subjective disaster in which all sense of remaining in being as the same person moment to moment, from day to day—one's very ipseity (Jaspers, 1913)—is obliterated and vanishes. Clearly, such a catastrophic loss will inevitably disrupt the temporal structure of the person's experience in general. Or, take the dimension of self–other differentiation, one on which ordinarily the person maintains an experiential boundary defining and delineating "I" and "Not-I." When this boundary dissolves—a calamity often accompanied by a terrifying feeling of melting into or being swallowed up by one's surroundings—all sense of the enduring solidity and separateness of reality is undermined. A third example I could offer involves the dimension of affectivity. Self-loss here means the disappearance of all sense of emotional aliveness as instead a feeling of infinite inner deadness arises at the core of one's Being. You may remember that Grace, whose life and therapy were described in Chapter 2, experienced this deadness following the collapse of her dream of becoming a nun and a missionary. The deadness was without limit and unendurable—she tried to control it by consuming vast amounts of alcohol. Grace was able to tell me a little about her overall experience of the world at that time. She said nothing seemed completely real—other people appeared to be at a great distance or to be robots mechanically functioning without meaning. She was experiencing a world-encompassing derealization and depersonalization. So, for every form and variation of the annihilation of the individual's subjective selfhood, there will be a co-occurring disintegration of his or her world.

RDS: A good example of this co-occurrence can be found in the experience of a traumatic loss. Such trauma dismantles one's sense of identity or self-continuity. But traumatic or tragic loss also creates a dark region in the topography of one's world that will always be there. A wave of profound sadness descends upon us whenever we step into such a region of loss. There, we are left adrift in a world hollowed out, emptied of light. It is a bleak region that can never be completely eradicated or cordoned off. The injunction to "let it go and move on" is thus an absurdity. There will always be "portkeys"[1] back into the darkness—the dark realm in which we need to be emotionally held so that the loss can be better borne and integrated.

GEA: Your thought, Bob, highlights the utter interdependence of self- and world-experience. Extreme trauma has a way of doing that, bringing forth into clarity fundamental features of our Being. I can add the following to your account. Every emotionally significant loss that a human being suffers not only threatens the sense of continuity, but also the very unity of the soul. Whom one has been in a world that included the beloved is not the same individual one becomes in a world from which the beloved has vanished. The agonies of mourning are the effects in our experience of the journey from the one to the other. Sometimes the transition is too difficult to complete, and a fissure appears between the "I" of the past and the "I" of the present and future. The former remains locked in a mystical embrace with the one who has vanished, while the latter moves on. This is the story of the great philosopher Søren Kierkegaard, who spoke of a "great earthquake" that followed a succession of devastating losses of beloved family members (Atwood, Stolorow, and Orange, 2011).

RDS: I am seeing the possibility of a wide range of phenomenological studies of very severe emotional disturbances, focusing on different self–world relationships and their constitutive relational contexts.

GEA: Yes, and although a significant beginning has been made in the works of our forebears—I would list Jung, Federn, Winnicott, Searles, Sullivan, Des Lauriers, Laing, among others—we are still at the beginning of our explorations of this strange and difficult country.

RDS: What held our antecedents back, by and large, was their continuing entanglement, each in his own way, with Cartesian theoretical concepts. Only Laing tried to be as radically phenomenological as you and me.

GEA: Laing's early work, *The Divided Self* (1959), is a work of genius as far as I am concerned, and it should be required reading for every clinician. Many of his later writings, I think, display a shocking concreteness that subverted his original phenomenological ideas. Laing succumbed to the reifying impulse that afflicts everyone who works in this field, including you and me. This is seen in the case of Laing most clearly in his book *The Facts of Life* (1976), wherein he traces the patterns one sees in the life of the person back to the misadventures of the fertilized egg as it seeks to implant itself in the uterine wall. Such concreteness has no place in a phenomenological contextualism!

RDS: As we chronicled in the first chapter, Ludwig Binswanger and Medard Boss were two additional early pioneers who saw the value of Heidegger's existential phenomenology for psychotherapy and psychoanalysis. They both proceeded "from the top down"—that is, they started with Heidegger's philosophical delineation of essential existential structures (Being-in-the-world, care, authenticity-inauthenticity, *das Man*, thrownness, existential anxiety, existential guilt, potentialities-for-Being, etc.) and applied these to clinical phenomena and the therapeutic situation. Although Binswanger's (1946) existential analysis produced some brilliant phenomenological descriptions of the "world-designs" (p. 195) underlying various forms of psychopathology, and Boss's (1963) Daseinsanalysis freed the psychoanalytic theory of therapy from the dehumanizing causal-mechanistic assumptions of Freudian metapsychology, neither effort brought about a radicalization of psychoanalytic practice itself or of the psychoanalytic process.

The evolution of our post-Cartesian psychoanalytic perspective (Stolorow, Atwood, and Orange, 2002), by contrast, proceeded "from the bottom up." It was born of our studies of the subjective origins of psychoanalytic theories and developed out of our concurrent efforts to rethink psychoanalysis as a form of phenomenological inquiry and to illuminate the phenomenology of the psychoanalytic process itself. Our dedication to phenomenological inquiry, in turn, led us to a contextualist theoretical perspective, and we subsequently found philosophical support in Heidegger's existential analytic for what we had illuminated.

GEA: What do you make of how our perspective has in general been isolated from other relational perspectives in psychoanalysis?

RDS: Clearly, our intersubjective-systems perspective, as its name suggests, has been a relational one since its early beginnings (Atwood and Stolorow, 1984). Upon reflection, however, I have realized that there is something about the development of our relational perspective that distinguishes it from most others. Typically, contemporary relational viewpoints have their origins in prior psychoanalytic *theories*—Sullivan's, Klein's, Fairbairn's, etc.—theories that contain concepts that are instantiations of Cartesian isolated-mind thinking. Concepts such as parataxic distortion, projective identification, and endopsychic structures are imported more or less uncritically into the corresponding contemporary relational viewpoints. In contrast, our perspective evolved from considerations of *method*—namely, our commitment to rethinking psychoanalysis as a form of phenomenological inquiry. This assiduous dedication to illuminating personal phenomenology led us from mind to world and thus from mental contents to relational contexts, from the intrapsychic to the intersubjective. From our phenomenological perspective, all of the clinical phenomena with which psychoanalysis has been traditionally concerned were seen as taking form within systems of interacting, differently organized, mutually influencing subjective worlds.

GEA: You have often claimed that phenomenology led us inexorably to contextualism, but you have never really explained this inexorability.

RDS: The central reason, I have come to realize, is that a psychoanalytic phenomenology, as opposed to other forms of phenomenological inquiry, is always devoted to investigating affectivity—that is, worlds of *emotional* experience. During the period we were fleshing out our psychoanalytic phenomenology, I was working on an article with Daphne Socarides Stolorow (Socarides and Stolorow, 1984/1985) in which we were suggesting that Kohut's central clinical contributions pertained essentially to affective experience. Furthermore, the experience of affect was grasped in this article as being inseparable from the contexts of attunement and malattunement in which it is felt. This understanding became seamlessly woven into the fabric of psychoanalytic phenomenology. The shift in focus from the primacy of drive to the primacy of affectivity moves psychoanalysis toward a phenomenological contextualism and a central focus on dynamic intersubjective systems. Unlike drives, which are claimed to originate deep within the interior of a Cartesian isolated mind, affect—subjective emotional experience—is something that from birth onward is co-constituted within ongoing relational systems. Therefore, locating affect at its center automatically entails a radical contextualization of virtually all aspects of human psychological life and of the psychoanalytic process.

For example, the focus on affect contextualizes the very boundary between conscious and unconscious. Unlike the Freudian repression barrier, viewed as a fixed intrapsychic structure within an isolated Cartesian container, the limiting horizons of emotional experiencing are conceptualized as emergent properties of ongoing dynamic intersubjective systems. Forming and evolving within a nexus of living systems, the horizons of experiencing are grasped as fluid and ever-shifting, products both of the person's unique intersubjective history and of what is or is not allowed to be felt within the intersubjective fields that constitute his or her current living.

A consistently phenomenological approach has also been especially fruitful in the effort to grasp the context-embeddedness of emotional trauma. Developmental trauma originates within a formative intersubjective context whose central feature is malattunement to painful affect—a breakdown of the child-caregiver interaffective system, leading to the child's loss of affect-integrating capacity and thereby to an unbearable, overwhelmed, disorganized state. Painful or frightening affect becomes traumatic when the context of emotional understanding—the "relational home"—that the child needs to assist in its tolerance and integration is profoundly absent. As we will develop in a later chapter, such contexts of developmental trauma are where pathogenesis takes form. We have shown that the intersubjective context plays a constitutive role in all forms of pathogenesis and in all aspects of the psychoanalytic process. Emotional phenomenology and relationality form an indissoluble unity, because relationality is constitutive of emotional experience.

GEA: It can be asked, doesn't a phenomenological-contextual account of trauma have to be grounded in something more fundamental, some form of solid bedrock—in other words, in a metaphysical entity? In an Age of Scientism, the metaphysical impulse typically turns to neuroscience in search of such grounding entities.

RDS: I know you already know my answer, George, which is contained in our critique of "the self." Metaphysical entities—neurological, psychiatric, and otherwise—cover up devastating contexts, replacing the tragic finitude and transience of human life with a reassuring picture of encapsulated, substantialized, and enduring realities. A perspective on emotional trauma that is phenomenological-contextual all the way down, by contrast, embraces the unbearable vulnerability and context-dependence of human existence. Such an embrace lies at the heart of an ethics of finitude and the comportment of emotional dwelling that is its condition of possibility. Phenomenological contextualism all the way down!

GEA: Let's take up a broader question now, pertaining to the nature of our collaboration over the years, and what it is that has made our intellectual relationship so productive for both of us. What would you say has been the secret of our success? You used to say about us that we have been so close to each other that we are actually the same person. My wife Elizabeth Atwood, upon hearing this insane statement, quipped: "Well, it is true that if you took Bob Stolorow and George Atwood and added them together, you would get *almost* one whole person!" If we were the same individual, however, our thoughts would have been identically the same—this has obviously not been the case.

RDS: The key to our productivity, George, extending now over almost 50 years and nine co-authored books (and countless articles), lies in how the similarities and differences in our individual perspectives have combined and interacted. In the second edition of our *Structures of Subjectivity* (Atwood and Stolorow, 2014), we characterized this process as dialectical in form.

GEA: Yes, from the beginning, one of us comes up with an idea or perspective, the other embraces it with enthusiasm but proposes some contrasting thought or viewpoint, and in the ensuing discussion the two contributions are brought together in a more inclusive structure. We differ, but never disagree. Apparent disagreements are always dealt with by searching for the integrating idea that will reveal a common ground. This is in dramatic contrast to the place in which we often find ourselves with so many colleagues in our field—our disagreements there are frequently absolute and there is no common ground that can be uncovered. We especially have such clashes with those who remain committed to a Cartesian worldview, often not recognizing their philosophical assumptions.

RDS: I could add that our intellectual comradeship is mirrored by a personal one, never marred by irreconcilable conflict, always supportive of each other even as each of us has passed through terrible crises and losses.

GEA: I asked a friend who knows both of us quite well what she thought the differences were between us. She answered instantly: "Bob Stolorow is a logic machine, George Atwood listens to the mermaids." Another friend of mine at Rutgers who has studied all our writings made the same point, comparing us to the main characters in the television program, *The X-Files*. He said Atwood is Mulder and Stolorow is Scully. I happen to know that you too sometimes hear the mermaids (indeed, you can be an incurable romantic!) and you know that I can occasionally run circles around people with a logical analysis. This is a difference that is only a matter of our most salient qualities, but it may be reflected in the essays we are dialoguing about. Your Credo is quite abstract, laying out an elegant structure of philosophical and theoretical assumptions, and developing their clinical applications. My Credo wanders all over the place, telling stories drawn from the realm of madness, imagining bright futures, and challenging clinicians to look deeply into their own souls.

RDS: The commonalities between our lives, George, are legion. We both developed an early interest in psychoanalysis in our teens, we both wanted to become psychiatrists, we both hit walls in pursuing our premedical and medical programs, we both fell back into doctoral studies in clinical psychology as an alternative, and we both were drawn during our student days to philosophical phenomenology and existential psychoanalysis. But we are far from carbon copies of one another.

GEA: Another area of quite profound difference is briefly taken up in my Credo chapter, in the section entitled, "The lost childhood of the therapist." In that section, I describe two pathways from childhood trauma and deprivation to a career as a psychotherapist. In one of these, the child becomes a caregiver who fills the emotional voids in the life of a depressed or otherwise disturbed parent. In the other, the child undergoes a loss of a beloved parent and repairs the broken bond through identification with that parent. Psychotherapists whose lives exemplify the first of these I called "Type 1 clinicians," whereas those following the second pathway are "Type 2 clinicians." I classify myself as a definite Type 2, with the central loss being that of my mother when I was 8 years old.

RDS: When you first told me of these ideas, I saw myself as "a mild case of Type 1," having given much of myself in my early years to trying to enliven and support my mother, who was periodically subject to severe wooden depressions. It was complicated though, because she oscillated between emotional deadness and loving responsiveness, and I alternated accordingly between feeling safe and connected on the one side, and alone and abandoned on the other.

GEA: Identifying with my mother who died, I became maternal, nurturant, a rescuer of deserted children, a refuge for the lost and the insane. The downside of the extremity to which this theme was carried in my life appeared in a self-sacrifice that sometimes went very far.

RDS: And my love of psychoanalytic investigation is, in part, heir to my lifelong search for my mother's emotional aliveness, hidden behind a wall of depressive inaccessibility. Illuminating meanings is a way to bring light into the darkness.

GEA: It can be said then that, in becoming psychoanalytic therapists, each of us found a means of restoring life and overcoming abandonment and death.

Note

1 I use the phrase *portkeys to trauma* to capture the profound impact of emotional trauma on our experience of time.

5

EMOTIONAL DISTURBANCE, TRAUMA, AND AUTHENTICITY

A phenomenological-contextualist perspective

Robert D. Stolorow

Phenomenological psychopathology

Beginning with its origins in the work of Karl Jaspers (1913), phenomenological psychopathology has traditionally been an investigation of the experiential worlds associated with particular mental disorders or psychiatric entities. The subtitle of a recently-published anthology on the subject (Stanghellini and Aragona, 2016) makes this focus explicit: *What is it Like to Suffer from Mental Disorders?* Of the 18 chapters between the introductory and concluding ones, 12 explicitly name a psychiatric diagnosis in their title. As is typical of such studies, the validity of this diagnosing is left unchallenged.

A particularly good example of this tradition in phenomenological psychopathology is provided by a recent book by Matthew Ratcliffe (2015), and I will be referring to it throughout this chapter. Central to his perspective is a conception of the experiential world as a space of possibilities and a distinction between intentional feelings—those that are about a particular intentional object—and pre-intentional feelings—those that indicate the kinds of intentional states that are possible within an experiential world. The latter, what Ratcliffe calls *existential feelings* (see also Ratcliffe, 2008), disclose the existential structure of experience, one's pre-intentional ways of finding oneself in the world. Ratcliffe's book—and here is its highly valuable contribution—is a study of changes in existential feeling—shifts and disturbances in the kinds of possibility that experience incorporates. His particular focus is the loss or diminution of kinds of possibility. One such loss that figures prominently in Ratcliffe's analysis is the loss of existential hope—the loss of a sense of the future as a domain of possible meaningful change for the better. Such pre-intentional existential hopelessness entails loss of the very basis for particular intentional hopes. Particular hopes and aspirations themselves become unintelligible, as the world is emptied of significance. Existential hopelessness emerges in Ratcliffe's analysis as a richly variegated, multidimensional unity. It can include a sense of eternal incarceration and irrevocable guilt. The sense of freedom of will and personal agency is often diminished or lost, and there is an accompanying alteration in the felt bodily "I can." Perhaps most important, existential hopelessness entails a profound alteration of temporality, the lived experience of time. Instead of being a linear unfolding toward an open future marked by possibility, time is felt to be circular, with a closed future characterized by endless repetition. Lastly, there is a feeling of profound alienation from others deriving from a sense of living in a reality different from that inhabited by everyone else.

Ratcliffe's analysis of the unity of existential hopelessness is quite elegant and very valuable. Would that he had stopped with that, rather than linking it with traditional psychiatric diagnosing! But he presents it to us as a phenomenological account of "experiences of depression," the unfortunate title of his book. But what is this "depression," the phenomenology of whose experiences he gives us? At several points he acknowledges that the word refers to something that is very heterogeneous and of questionable empirical validity. Correspondingly, he cautions against associating specific forms of experience with specific diagnostic categories. It does not help to claim that depression is an "ideal type," as Ratcliffe does, because he continues to refer to it as if it were a psychiatric entity or illness (he does the same with schizophrenia), a condition with particular symptoms from which it can be diagnosed. After commenting on the inadequacy and questionable validity of psychiatry's *Diagnostic and Statistical Manual of Mental Disorders* (*DSM*) (American Psychiatric Association, 2013), Ratcliffe proceeds to use two of its categories—"major depressive episode" and "major depressive disorder"—as the organizing psychiatric framework for his studies.

Recent research has called into question the most recent *DSM*'s creation of new diagnostic entities and categories that are scientifically unsubstantiated and that over-pathologize vulnerable populations such as young children, the elderly, and the traumatically bereaved (Frances, 2013). More fundamentally, the *DSM* is a direct descendent of Descartes's (1641) metaphysical dualism, which divided the finite world into two distinct basic substances—*res cogitans* and *res extensa*, thinking substances (minds) with no extension in space, and extended substances (bodies and other material things) that do not think. This metaphysical dualism concretized the idea of a complete separation between mind and world, between subject and object. What, after all, could be more separate than two realms of being constituted by two completely different substances? Descartes's vision can be characterized as a radical decontextualization of both mind and world. Mind, the "thinking thing," is isolated from the world in which it dwells, just as the world is purged of all human significance. Both mind and world are stripped of all contextuality with respect to one another, as they are beheld in their bare thinghood, their pure presence-at-hand, as Heidegger (1927) would say. The ontological gap between mind and world, between subject and object, is bridged only in a relationship of thinking, in which the "worldless subject" somehow forms ideas that more or less accurately represent or correspond to transcendent (i.e., mind-independent) objects in an "unworlded world."

The *DSM* partakes of what might be called *the illusion of perceptible essences* (see Chapter 6). Wittgenstein (1953) explained how such an illusion is constituted by the use of a single word to denote an array of items that bear a "family resemblance" to one another—i.e., items that share some qualities but not others. When such items are grouped together under one word, a reified picture is created of an essence that each of them instantiates. The *DSM* will present several symptoms that are claimed to be characteristic of a diagnostic entity, say depression, and a patient—or better, the patient's mind—is said to be afflicted with this disorder if a certain proportion of those symptoms are manifest. That is, people whose sufferings bear a family resemblance to one another become, through the reified picture that has been named, instantiations of a metaphysical diagnostic essence, a disordered Cartesian mind.

In his existential analytic, Heidegger (1927) seeks interpretively to re-find the unity of our being, split asunder in the Cartesian bifurcation. Thus, what he calls the "destruction" of traditional ontology is a clearing away of its concealments and disguises, in order to unveil the primordial contextual whole that it has been covering up. His contextualism is formally indicated early on, in his designation of the human being as *Dasein*, to-be-there or to-be-situated, a term that already points to the unity of the human kind of being and its context. This initially-indicated contextualization is to be further fleshed out as Heidegger focuses his hermeneutic-phenomenological inquiry, with its contextualist interpretive perspective, on our average everyday understanding of our kind of Being. His aim is to "lay bare a fundamental structure in Dasein: Being-in-the-world" (Heidegger, 1927, p. 65), also described as Dasein's "basic state" (constitution) or "constitutive state" (p. 78). In introducing the idea of Being-in-the-world, Heidegger makes clear both that he has arrived at it through hermeneutic inquiry and that his interpretive perspective is a contextualist or holistic one: "In the *interpretation of Dasein*, this structure is something '*a priori*'; it is not pieced together, but is *primordially and constantly a whole*" (p. 65, emphasis added).

With the hyphens unifying the expression *Being-in-the-world* (*In-der-Welt-sein*), Heidegger indicates that, in his interpretation of Dasein, the traditional ontological gap between our Being and our world is to be definitively closed and that, in their indissoluble unity, our Being and our world "primordially and constantly" always contextualize one another. Heidegger's ontological contextualism, in which human being is saturated with the world in which we dwell and the world we inhabit is drenched in human meanings and purposes, provides a solid philosophical grounding for a *psychoanalytic phenomenological contextualism* (Atwood and Stolorow, 2014), replacing the Cartesian isolated mind that underpins both traditional diagnostic psychiatry and classical Freudian psychoanalysis.

The *DSM* is a pseudo-scientific manual for diagnosing disordered Cartesian isolated minds. As such, it completely overlooks the exquisite context-sensitivity and radical context-dependence of human emotional life and of all forms of emotional disturbance. Against the *DSM*, Atwood and I (Atwood and Stolorow, 2014) have contended that all emotional disturbances are constituted in a context of human interrelatedness—specifically, contexts of emotional trauma. One such traumatizing context is characterized by relentless invalidation of emotional experience, coupled with an objectification of the child as being intrinsically defective—a trauma that is readily repeated in the experience of being psychiatrically diagnosed. This retraumatization, in turn, can actually co-constitute the manifest clinical picture.[1] Ratcliffe elaborates a phenomenological account of existential hopelessness that invites exploration and appreciation of its context-embeddedness, but he encases it in an objectifying psychiatric diagnostic language that negates this very embeddedness! I contend that this criticism holds for the field of phenomenological psychopathology in general.

Existential anxiety and emotional trauma

Ratcliffe notes an important similarity between his characterization of existential hopelessness and Heidegger's phenomenological description of existential anxiety (*Angst*), in which the everyday world becomes devoid of practical significance. In Heidegger's ontological *account* of anxiety, which Ratcliffe does not discuss, the central features of its phenomenology—the collapse of everyday significance and the resulting feelings of uncanniness, of not being at home in the everyday world—are claimed to be grounded in what Heidegger called authentic (non-evasively owned) *Being-toward-death*. Death, in this account, is a distinctive possibility that is constitutive of our existence—of our intelligibility to ourselves in our futurity and our finitude.

In my own work (Stolorow, 2007, 2011), I have contended that emotional trauma produces an affective state whose features bear a close similarity to the central elements in Heidegger's existential interpretation of anxiety, and that it accomplishes this by plunging the traumatized person into a form of authentic Being-toward-death. Trauma shatters the illusions of everyday life that evade and cover up the finitude, contingency, and embeddedness of our existence and the indefiniteness of its certain extinction. Such shattering exposes what had been heretofore concealed, thereby plunging the traumatized person into a form of authentic Being-toward-death and into the anxiety—the loss of significance, the uncanniness—through which authentic Being-toward-death is disclosed. My description of trauma's impact in disrupting our experience of time and our connectedness with others is remarkably similar to the corresponding features that Ratcliffe attributes to existential hopelessness. Trauma, I contended, devastatingly disrupts the ordinary, average-everyday linearity of temporality, the sense of stretching along from the past to an open future. Experiences of emotional trauma become freeze-framed into an eternal present in which one remains forever trapped or to which one is condemned to be perpetually returned. In the region of trauma, all duration or stretching along collapses, the traumatic past becomes present, and future loses all meaning other than endless repetition. Because trauma so profoundly modifies the universal or shared structure of temporality, I claimed, the traumatized person quite literally lives in another kind of reality, an experiential world felt to be incommensurable with those of others. This felt incommensurability, in turn, contributes to the sense of alienation and estrangement from other human beings that typically haunts the traumatized person. Experiences of severe emotional trauma are the contexts, concealed by Ratcliffe's devotion to a decontextualizing psychiatric language, in which the existential feelings that he so beautifully elucidates take form. And, not accidentally, these same contexts of severe trauma are those in which the emotional disturbances that are objectified by the *DSM* also take form (Atwood, 2011). There are no diagnostic entities, only devastating contexts.

What enables us to exist authentically—that is, to own our Being-toward-death and to bear the existential anxiety that such owning entails? Heidegger does not tell us, but the phenomenology of trauma and the relational contexts that facilitate its transformation contain clues as to what makes authenticity possible.

I have contended that emotional trauma can be borne to the extent that it finds a context of emotional understanding—what I call a *relational home*—in which it can be held. In a sense, in the context of a receptive and understanding relational home, traumatized states can cease to be traumatic, or at least cease to be enduringly so. Within such a relational home, traumatized states are in a process of becoming less severely traumatic—i.e., of becoming less overwhelming and more bearable—thus making evasive defenses less necessary. Thus, within a holding relational home, the traumatized person may become able to move toward more authentic (non-evasive) existing. Authenticity as a possibility in the wake of trauma, I am proposing, is embedded in a broader contextual whole within which traumatized states can evolve into painful emotional experiences that can be more fully felt and articulated, better tolerated, and eventually integrated. Authentic existing presupposes a capacity to live in the emotional pain (e.g., the existential anxiety) that accompanies a non-evasive experience of finitude, and this capacity, in turn, requires that such pain find a relational context in which it can be held.[2]

The counterpart of inauthenticity in the phenomenology of trauma is called *dissociation*, a defensive process discussed by most authors on trauma. I think of defensive dissociation phenomenologically as a kind of *tunnel vision*—a narrowing of one's experiential horizons so as to exclude and evade the terrifying, the prohibited, and the emotionally unbearable. Such narrowing of one's horizons entails the keeping apart of incommensurable emotional worlds, a process that contributes to the devastating impact of emotional trauma on our experience of temporality. I use the term *portkey*, which I borrowed from *Harry Potter and the Goblet of Fire* (Rowling, 2000), to capture the profound impact of emotional trauma on our experience of time. Harry was a severely traumatized little boy, nearly killed by his parents' murderer and left in the care of a family that mistreated him cruelly. He arose from the ashes of devastating trauma as a wizard in possession of wondrous magical powers, and yet never free from the original trauma, always under threat by his parents' murderer. As a wizard, he encountered portkeys—objects that transported him instantly to other places, obliterating the duration ordinarily required for travel from one location to another.[3] Portkeys to trauma return one again and again to an experience of traumatization. The experience of such portkeys fractures, and can even obliterate, one's sense of unitary selfhood, of Being-in-time.

The endless recurrence of emotional trauma is ensured by the finitude of our existence and the finitude of all those we love.[4] Authentic temporality, insofar as it owns up to human finitude, is traumatic temporality. *Trauma recovery* is an oxymoron—human finitude with its traumatizing impact is not an illness from which one can recover, and innocence lost cannot be regained. "Recovery" is a misnomer for the constitution of an expanded emotional world that coexists alongside the absence of the one that has been shattered by trauma. The expanded world and the absent shattered world may be more or less integrated or dissociated, depending on the degree to which the unbearable emotional pain evoked by the traumatic shattering has become integrated or remains dissociated defensively, which depends in turn on the extent to which such pain found a relational home in which it could be held. This is the essential fracturing at the heart of traumatic temporality. From this perspective, authenticity may be understood as a relative ease of passage between the expanded world and the shattered world of trauma.

Authentic existing that seizes and affirms its own nullity must bear the dark foreboding that accompanies it as the signature affect of traumatic temporality. I have contended (Stolorow, 2007, 2011) that the darkness can be enduringly borne only in relational contexts of deep emotional attunement and understanding. This contention has crucial implications for the therapeutic approach to emotional trauma.

Therapeutic implications

I have been moving toward a more active, relationally engaged form of therapeutic comportment that I call *emotional dwelling*. In dwelling, one does not merely seek empathically to understand the other's emotional pain from the other's perspective. One does that, but much more. In dwelling, one leans into the other's emotional pain and participates in it, perhaps with the aid of one's own analogous experiences of pain. I have found that this active, engaged, participatory comportment is especially important in the therapeutic approach to emotional trauma. The language that one uses to address another's experience of emotional trauma meets the trauma head-on, articulating the unbearable and the unendurable, saying the unsayable, unmitigated by any efforts to soothe, comfort, encourage, or reassure—such efforts invariably being experienced by the other as a shunning or turning away from his or her traumatized state.

If we are to be an understanding relational home for a traumatized person, we must tolerate, even draw upon, our own existential vulnerabilities so that we can dwell unflinchingly with his or her unbearable and recurring emotional pain. When we dwell with others' unendurable pain, their shattered emotional worlds are enabled to shine with a kind of sacredness that calls forth an understanding and caring engagement within which traumatized states can be gradually transformed into bearable and nameable painful feelings.

What is it in our existential structure that makes the offering and the finding of a relational home for emotional trauma possible? I have contended (Stolorow, 2007, 2011) that, just as finitude and vulnerability to death and loss are fundamental to our existential constitution, so too is it constitutive of our existence that we meet each other as "brothers and sisters in the same dark night" (Vogel, 1994, p. 97), deeply connected with one another in virtue of our *common* finitude. Thus, although the possibility of emotional trauma is ever-present, so too is the possibility of forming bonds of deep emotional attunement within which devastating emotional pain can be held, rendered more tolerable, and, hopefully, eventually integrated. Our existential kinship-in-the-same-darkness is the condition for the possibility both of the profound contextuality of emotional trauma and of the mutative power of human understanding. I suggest, as does Vogel (1994), that owning up to our existential kinship-in-finitude has significant implications for what might be called an *ethics of finitude*, insofar as it motivates us, or even obligates us, to care about and for our brothers' and sisters' existential vulnerability and emotional pain.

Concluding remarks

I have presented a critique of traditional phenomenological psychopathology for failing to challenge and move beyond traditional diagnostic psychiatry and its Cartesian isolated-mind thinking. Such objectifying thinking obscures the embeddedness of emotional disturbances in constitutive contexts of emotional trauma. There are no psychiatric entities, I have contended, only traumatic contexts. And I have shown that Heidegger's existential analytic provides not only a philosophical grounding for a psychoanalytic phenomenological contextualism but also a pathway for grasping the existential meanings of emotional trauma.

What would phenomenological psychopathology look like if it were to incorporate my criticisms and claims? On one hand, it would illuminate the dimensions of emotional worlds that are disrupted and altered in particular forms of emotional disturbance. Ratcliffe (2015), as I have said, has provided an excellent example of such phenomenological description in his analysis of existential hopelessness. On the other hand, it would seek to identify the particular contexts of emotional trauma—not psychiatric diagnoses!—that are implicated in the formation of these disturbed emotional worlds. Without reified psychiatric entities and with a focus on contexts of emotional trauma, phenomenological psychopathology could become more relevant to psychoanalytic therapy and more truly phenomenological!

Dialogue

GEA: Isn't it the case, Bob, that adopting a consistently phenomenological perspective undermines the very concept of psychopathology?

RDS: Yes it does, if we understand the term "pathology" as referring to conditions wholly internal to a person, stripped of their constitutive contexts. "Mental illnesses," "psychological disorders," diagnostic "entities" of any and all kinds vanish without a trace.

GEA: The task of diagnosis accordingly is transformed and made much more complex, refocused on describing different worlds of experience, according to the subjective themes they show with the greatest salience. Those worlds, in all their variations, are in turn conceptualized as inseparably embedded in intersubjective contexts that have to be included in any diagnosis that takes place.

RDS: Adhering to pseudo-scientific ideas about so-called mental illness obstructs phenomenological investigation by fixing our attention on departures in our patients' experiences and behaviors from an imagined ideal of normality. The deviations from the ideal are then redefined as symptoms emanating from the inside of someone, blinding the clinical observer to the embeddedness of what he or she is seeing in its constitutive context.

GEA: I think clinicians need to think about the impact on their patients of being observed and categorized within a traditional diagnostic framework. They should think as well of the very different effects of being regarded phenomenologically and intersubjectively.

RDS: The effect of someone coming to us with an interest in our experiences and their contexts is generally one of feeling understood; the impact of being viewed as mentally ill, by contrast, most often involves a sense of being critically evaluated and objectified.

GEA: Consider what it is like, as a particular example, to be diagnosed as "schizophrenic." For a person who is already experiencing grave difficulties in maintaining a sense of his or her own selfhood and emotional world, such a diagnosis can be utterly annihilating in its impact. I once had a patient who came to me after having been aggressively confronted by her psychiatrist with this very diagnosis—the doctor had told her she was required to take antipsychotic medications for life, due to her ultimately incurable illness. She felt invalidated and defined by this declaration, and began to have sensations of a mysterious physical defect materializing at the center of her brain. She begged me to explain to her what this "schizophrenia" was, and what was wrong inside her brain. I saw how the diagnostic attribution had invaded and usurped her very precarious sense of herself and decided to try to reverse this awful effect. I said to her that I was going to tell her a secret and hoped she would listen to me. I told her that the entire diagnostic system in psychiatry was unscientific and bankrupt, and she should disregard what her doctor had so forcefully presented. I said it was pure B.S. But I did not stop there. This patient had also given me an account of recent events in her life that had been massively destabilizing. So, I simply said that she had been through hell in the last weeks and everything had fallen apart. Just that, and nothing more—except to reiterate that she did not have an incurable illness and also to say there was no reason she could not recover and get things together. She smiled after I said all this, answering: "I think you and I are going to get along well." I worked with her for the next three decades and she did well.

RDS: That is such a wonderful example, George, one in which we can compare and contrast the very different effects of a pathologizing diagnostic attitude on the one side, and a phenomenological-contextualist perspective on the other. The phenomenological description you gave your patient appears to have been therapeutic in its effect.

GEA: There is nothing more powerfully therapeutic than the experience of being understood. Compare that with the terrible destructiveness of a diagnostic objectification. Here is a story about a young man I shall call John who committed suicide in consequence of being told of his diagnosis. The man, a student and the roommate of another gentleman who was my patient, had been in an ongoing emotional crisis for months and was in danger of failing out of college. Among his many symptoms, there were increasingly violent mood swings, oscillating between dark despair and episodes of euphoric hypomania. John, at the urging of his mother, made an appointment at a local mental health center and was interviewed there by a psychiatric resident. The interview covered his difficulties with his college studies, a recent breakup with a girlfriend, and a traumatic history in his family of origin. His father had himself been emotionally unstable, and had repeatedly disrupted family life with his own manic-depressive pattern of alternating mood states. The father had been, according to the account given, a "demon from Hell," one who had utterly destroyed the peace and stability of life in the home. The psychiatrist, looking at his patient's current struggles and hearing of this family history, said: "The diagnosis is clear, John, and it is confirmed by your genetic background: you have bipolar disorder. This illness is treatable, and I will be prescribing mood stabilizing medications that you will need to be taking indefinitely." John listened to his doctor, thanked him for his honesty, and left the clinic with his prescription. I know about what transpired here because John spoke briefly to his roommate, my patient, about his meeting with the psychiatrist. John felt that he had been told that he was destined to be his father once more, afflicted with a mental disease that doomed him to become another demon from Hell. Later that day, he hanged himself. He left a note explaining his decision.

RDS: That is a terrible story, George! The psychiatrist evidently thought he was providing information regarding his patient's mental illness, and did not think about what it might feel like to be given this diagnosis—especially in view of the history with the father. That failure appears to have cost this patient his life. How might you, George, have handled this situation differently?

GEA: A terrible story indeed, Bob, and one that deeply hurt my patient, John's roommate, who did not anticipate his friend's death and blamed himself for not having foreseen the catastrophe. If I had been the interviewing clinician, I am certain I would not have told John he had the mental illness known as bipolar disorder. I might have noted the seeming correspondence between the mood disturbances of John and his father and wondered whether John himself was frightened by any perceived resemblance. It has been my experience that the children of severely disturbed parents are always afraid of repeating their parent's fate. I can picture something roughly similar to what I did with the patient who had been told she had schizophrenia. I would perhaps have told him that he should discount any family parallelisms he was imagining, and that I thought his emotional crisis was due to trauma—there had been a disastrous breakup with a girlfriend, and the family history was replete with traumatic disruptions going all the way back to John's earliest years. Trauma, I would have explained, is something that can be ameliorated, and it is not a mental illness one is doomed to suffer one's whole life long. I might also have expressed my view that the entire diagnostic system in psychiatry is bankrupt, based on an outmoded metaphysics, and not supported by convincing scientific evidence. I don't think a suicide would then have occurred, because there would have been no reason for it.

RDS: Let's turn from the extreme states called "psychotic" to more everyday patterns that often are diagnosed as character disorders.

GEA: Yes, let's widen the scope.

RDS: Traditionally, in psychology, psychiatry, and psychoanalysis, the term *character* has been used to refer to constellations or configurations of behavioral traits: "anal characters" are said to be compulsive and perfectionist; "hysterical characters" are described as histrionic; "passive aggressive characters" show anger covertly by withholding; "narcissistic characters" are excessively self-centered; "borderline characters" form chaotic and primitive relationships; and so on.

How might character be understood from a phenomenological perspective like ours that takes organizations or worlds of emotional experiencing as its principal focus? We have long contended that such organizations of emotional experiencing always take form in contexts of human interrelatedness. Developmentally, recurring patterns of emotional interaction within the child–caregiver system give rise to principles (thematic patterns, meaning-structures, cognitive–emotional schemas) that shape subsequent emotional experiences, especially experiences of significant relationships. Such organizing principles are unconscious, not in the sense of being repressed, but in being pre-reflective. Ordinarily, we just have our experiences; we do not reflect on the principles or meanings that shape them.

The totality of a person's pre-reflective organizing principles, from our perspective, constitutes his or her character. From this perspective, there can be no character "types" that exist as decontextualized entities or metaphysical essences, since every person's array of organizing principles is unique and singular, a product of his or her unique life history. These organizing principles show up in virtually every significant aspect of a person's life—in one's recurring relationship patterns, vocational choices, political commitments, interests, creative activity, fantasies, dreams, and emotional disturbances. Psychoanalytic therapy is a dialogical method for bringing this pre-reflective organizing activity into reflective self-awareness—particularly as it colors the therapeutic relationship in the form of transference—so that, hopefully, it can be transformed.

GEA: Although there are no character types existing as isolated, decontextualized entities, there are typically recurring patterns of intersubjective transaction that one can classify and describe. The apparent rigidity of such patterns resides not in fixed intrapsychic structures, in our view, but rather in relatively stable configurations of intersubjective reciprocity that include the typical responses elicited from others in the relational surround. The study of such intersubjective patterns represents a vitally important area of clinical psychoanalytic research, one that has scarcely begun to be explored.

RDS: What would be the purpose of such research, George?

GEA: The purpose would be to illuminate the embeddedness of characterological patterns of experience in their constitutive contexts!

RDS: Perhaps a look at our understanding of developmental trauma will help here. Early contexts of emotional trauma have particularly important consequences for the development of character as we conceive of it. From our perspective, developmental trauma is viewed not as an instinctual flooding of an ill-equipped Cartesian container, as Freud (1926) would have it, but as an experience of unbearably painful emotion. Furthermore, the intolerability of an emotional state cannot be explained solely, or even primarily, on the basis of the quantity or intensity of the painful feelings evoked by an injurious event. Traumatic emotional states can be grasped only in terms of the relational systems in which they are felt (Stolorow and Atwood, 1992, Chapter 4). Developmental trauma originates within a formative relational context whose central feature is malattunement to painful emotion, a breakdown of the child–caregiver system leading to the child's loss of emotional integrating capacity and, thereby, to an unbearable, overwhelmed, disorganized state. Painful or frightening emotion becomes traumatic when the attunement that the child needs to assist in its tolerance and integration is profoundly absent. From the claim that trauma is constituted in a relational context wherein severe emotional pain cannot find an understating home in which it can be held, it follows that injurious childhood experiences in and of themselves need not be traumatic (or at least not lastingly so) or pathogenic, provided that they occur within a responsive milieu. *Pain is not pathology*. It is the absence of adequate attunement to the child's painful emotional reactions that renders them unendurable and, thus, a source of traumatic states and psychopathology. This conceptualization holds both for discrete, dramatic traumatic events and for the more subtle "cumulative traumas" (Khan, 1963) that occur continually throughout childhood. A parent's narcissistic use of the child, for example, may preclude the recognition of, acceptance of, and attuned responsiveness to the child's painful emotional states.

As I discussed in the previous chapter, one consequence of developmental trauma, relationally conceived, is that emotional states take on enduring, crushing meanings. From recurring experiences of malattunement (situations in which the child's feelings are ignored, rejected, invalidated, devalued, shamed, punished, and so on), the child acquires the unconscious conviction that unmet developmental yearnings and reactive painful feeling states are manifestations of a loathsome defect or of an inherent inner badness. A defensive self-ideal is often established, representing a self-image purified of the offending emotional states that were perceived to be unwelcome or damaging to caregivers. Living up to this emotionally purified ideal becomes a central requirement for maintaining harmonious ties to others and for upholding self-esteem. Thereafter, the emergence of prohibited emotion is experienced as a failure to embody the required ideal, an exposure of the underlying essential defectiveness or badness, and is accompanied by feelings of isolation, shame, and self-loathing. A person with such unconscious organizing principles will expect that his or her feelings will be met by others with disgust, disdain, disinterest, alarm, hostility, withdrawal, exploitation, and the like, or will damage others and destroy his or her relationships with them. For example, in the psychoanalytic situation, such expectations, often unwittingly confirmed by the analyst, are a powerful source of resistance to the experience and articulation of emotion. Intractable repetitive transferences and resistances can be grasped, from this perspective, as rigidly stable states of the patient–analyst system, in which the meanings of the analyst's stance have become tightly coordinated with the patient's grim expectations and fears, thereby exposing the patient repeatedly to threats of re-traumatization.

What happens to psychiatric diagnoses of character disorders in this understanding? They *disappear*, and are replaced by organizing themes formed in contexts of trauma and the impact of such experiences in shaping one's emotional world.

GEA: This is an excellent discussion of developmental trauma, Bob, and it is really quite revolutionary in its implications. The very concept of character or personality is called into question as the consistent themes of an individual's distinctive ways of being are recast as embedded in and constituted by intersubjective systems. Is the world ready for such a reconceptualization?

Notes

1 See Atwood (2011), Chapter 2.

2 I have suggested (Stolorow, 2011, Chapter 9) that, during the period when he was working on the ideas in *Being and Time*, Heidegger found such a relational home in his close bond with Hannah Arendt. When he looked into the abyss of nothingness, he had his sustaining muse at his side.

3 My wife, Dr. Julia Schwartz, first brought this imagery of portkeys to my attention, as a metaphor that captures the impact of trauma on the experience of temporality.

4 I have claimed (Stolorow, 2011) that authentic Being-toward-death entails owning up not only to one's own finitude, but also to the finitude of those we love. Hence, authentic Being-toward-death always includes Being-toward-loss as a central constituent. Just as, existentially, we are "always dying already" (Heidegger, 1927, p. 298), so too are we always already grieving. Death and loss are existentially equiprimordial. Existential anxiety anticipates both death and loss.

6

THE PHENOMENOLOGY OF LANGUAGE AND THE METAPHYSICALIZING OF THE REAL

Soon after beginning work on a project on the phenomenology of language, we came upon Andrew Inkpin's (2016) recent book, *Disclosing the World: On the Phenomenology of Language*. The title of the book alone left us wondering whether there is anything remaining for us to illuminate. Indeed, there is. Drawing on the works of Heidegger, Merleau-Ponty, and Wittgenstein, Inkpin presents an elegant and comprehensive account of how the experience of language and its principles of organization play a constitutive, usually prereflective role in disclosing and opening up the world. He does *not*, however, pay systematic attention to how the experience of language, in Wittgenstein's (1953) words, bewitches intelligence by playing a constitutive role in the formation of metaphysical illusion—the subject matter of this essay.

Wittgenstein's account of how language bewitches one's intelligence is a singular achievement in the phenomenology of language. In section 426 of *Philosophical Investigations*, Wittgenstein famously claims that the meaning of a word is to be found in the "actual use" of it, and he contrasts this understanding with the projection of a picture:

> A picture is conjured up which seems to fix the sense *unambiguously*. The actual use, compared with that suggested by the picture, seems like something muddied. . . . [T]he form of expression we use seems to have been designed for a god, who knows what we cannot know; he sees the whole of each of those infinite series and he sees into human consciousness.
>
> (Wittgenstein, 1953, section 426, p. 108)

Wittgenstein is claiming here that, when one projects a picture as the meaning of a word, it gives one the illusion of a God's-eye view of the word's referent as a thing-in-itself, an illusory clarity that one much prefers over the "muddied" view given in the understanding that the actual meaning of a word is to be found in its multiple and shifting contexts of use. When the illusory picture is then imagined as ultimately real, the word has become transformed into a metaphysical entity. In place of the "muddied" view given by contexts of use—finite, contingent, unstable, transient—one can imagine the clear outlines of an everlasting entity. Metaphysical illusion, mediated by reified pictures, replaces the finitude and transience of existence with a God's-eye view of an irreducibly absolute and eternally changeless reality (Stolorow and Atwood, 2013). A bewitchment of intelligence by language is thereby accomplished!

In what follows, we seek to expand Wittgenstein's analysis of bewitchment of intelligence by language into a broader account of how one's prereflective experience of language shapes one's sense of the real.

The illusion of spatial location

A good example, also discussed by Wittgenstein, is the use of words that properly describe geometric space to "locate" emotional experience. People speak of their *inner* experiences, their *inner* feelings, getting their anger (from the inside) *out*, taking things *in*, looking *inward* (introspection), etc. These expressions correspond to Descartes's picture of the mind as a thinking thing that has an inside with contents and that looks out upon an external world from which it is separated. The picture of the mind as an entity located in Cartesian space—a picture institutionalized in the experience of everyday language—reifies what Zahavi (2005) calls *experiential selfhood*, the "mineness" of one's experiences. Such a picture prereflectively transforms the vulnerable, context-dependent, and evanescent experience of mineness into the stability and clarity of geometric space.

The illusion of perceptible essences

Another example discussed by Wittgenstein is found in the use of a single word to denote an array of items that bear a "family resemblance" to one another—i.e., items that share some qualities but not others. When such items are grouped together under one word, a reified picture is created of an essence that each of them instantiates. Psychiatry's *Diagnostic and Statistical Manual*, for example, will present several symptoms that are claimed to be characteristic of a diagnostic entity, say depression, and a patient is said to be afflicted with this disorder if a certain proportion of those symptoms are manifest. That is, people whose sufferings bear a family resemblance to one another become, through the reified picture that has been named, instantiations of a metaphysical diagnostic essence, an essence that can somehow be directly perceived through some form of "eidetic intuition" (Husserl, 1900, 1913).

The illusion of transparency

Consider again, briefly, the word *mind*, a term showing a great many meanings, depending on its particular contexts of use. In one of these, a picture commonly visualized is of an entity having external boundaries and an interior with contents. As noted earlier, the spatial interiority of such a picture reifies and absolutizes the subjective sense of "minenesss," metaphysicalizing the experience of one's perceptions, thoughts, and feelings being one's own. When one thinks of oneself and others as possessing minds, something that may seem to be as incontrovertible as the proposition that the sun rises in the morning, experiential lives acquire a dimension of "inwardness" separating the experiencing subject from "outer" reality. In actual language use, the pictures accompanying the use of this word fluctuate, in a kind of dance of variations in which what is denoted and connoted, visualized and absolutized, shifts from moment to moment in synchrony with changes in its context.

Imagining the meaning of the term "mind" to coincide fully with its associated picture, one may also presuppose that this meaning is shared by others. The use of the word in conversation is accordingly regarded as transparent to the other, who is presumed to live in a common world and to be in contact with exactly that of which one speaks. But how can one know that the meaning of this term, and really of any word one uses, is the same for the other as it is for oneself?

Perhaps the illusion of transparency, of absolute equivalency of meaning, serves as an antidote to a painful sense of isolation accompanying the finitude of intersubjective relatedness. One person can never know with absolute certainty the experience of the other, the only possibility being a succession of ever-closer approximations. Could it be that by embracing universalized pictures of the meanings of the words one uses and diverting one's gaze from all the deficiencies and ambiguities in mutual understanding, one is shielded from an otherwise unbearable feeling of being alone?

The tragic and the metaphysical

The first Western philosopher to examine systematically the relationship between the tragedy of human finitude and the ubiquity of metaphysical illusion was Wilhelm Dilthey (1910). As is elegantly reconstructed by de Mul (2004), Dilthey's life's work can be seen as an effort to replace the Kantian *a priori*—the timeless forms of perception and categories of cognition through which the world becomes intelligible to us—with "life categories" that are historically contingent and constituted over the course of a living historical process. There is a tragic dimension to Dilthey's historical consciousness, in that it brings out the "tragic contradiction between the philosophical desire for universal validity [the metaphysical impulse] and the realization of the fundamental finitude of every attempt to satisfy that desire" (de Mul, 2004, p. 154). Dilthey's recognition of this tragic contradiction leads him to elaborate a hermeneutic phenomenology of metaphysics. Dilthey's historical reconstruction of the development of metaphysics aims at no less than its "euthanasia." Although he holds that metaphysical desire is inherent to human nature, what he seeks to unmask are the illusions that this ubiquitous desire creates. Metaphysical illusion, according to Dilthey, transforms historically contingent nexuses of intelligibility—worldviews, as he eventually calls them—into timeless forms of reality. Anticipating Heidegger (1927), Dilthey holds that every worldview is grounded in a mood regarding the tragic realization of the finitude of life. The metaphysicalization of worldviews transforms the unbearable fragility and transience of all things human into an enduring, permanent, changeless reality, an illusory world of eternal truths. Dilthey grasps the metaphysical impulse as a relentless tendency to transform the experience of the real—how entities are intelligible to us—into a reified vision of the REALLY real. In this chapter, we have contended that a certain feature of the phenomenology of language—the prereflective presumption that words refer to pictures and that the pictures depict metaphysical entities—plays a constitutive role in such illusory transformations.

Metaphysical illusion in everyday life

An understanding of the reified pictures that are associated with the words one uses leads to the idea that people generally are metaphysicians. Assuming that the words that are spoken have fixed, universally transparent meanings, one is lulled away from an anxious appreciation of the contingent, ever-shifting nature of intersubjective life. What are the interrelated dimensions of experience that are engaged in this metaphysicalization of everyday existence?

One of these is that of solidity: in other words, the sense of the tangible, of the physical, of the dense and heavy. If one's words have no fixed and absolute meanings, the very foundations on which one stands threaten to dissolve into thin air.

A second dimension is one of continuity, an experience of the sameness over time of the various things of which one speaks. The pictures evoked by the words that are used are of entities showing a reassuring stability from each moment to the next, offering protection against a descent into temporal chaos.

Still another dimension is that of coherence. The pictures that one assumes capture the meanings of what is said are of wholes, of parts that form a unity or identity that is felt to exist in its own right. Stripped of such coherence, all the things of one's world, including other people and one's own very selfhood, collapse into an unbearable indeterminacy.

What would happen to the human experience of language and communication if the reified pictures one imagines as the meanings of the words that are spoken, transparently available to all, vanished and were replaced by an ongoing sense of those words' fluidity as they are used in varying contexts? What if the felt certainties accompanying our verbal exchanges with one another melted into an ever-changing incoherence and insolidity? By metaphysicalizing the words and meanings of everyday discourse, human beings confer a calming order on their experiences of life and the language used symbolically to represent them. The very same linguistic capacities that make possible the disclosure of human finitude also provide the means by which the tragedy of finitude is evaded.

Concluding remarks

Most often, the term "finitude" is used to denote temporal limitedness—mortality. But the term can be seen to encompass all the ways in which finite human existing is limited, and each can be a source of traumatic emotion (Stolorow, 2007). For example, as we have noted, there is also the impossibility of clear and certain knowing and the corresponding finitude of intersubjective relatedness. Human beings must navigate these multiple dimensions of finitude, and they do so by creating a multitude of countervailing metaphysical illusions that serve to evade or counteract the corresponding traumatic affect. Far from being distinguished by being an *animal rationale*, the human being, as Dilthey recognized, is a being who cannot exist without metaphysical illusion, and such illusion, as Wittgenstein understood, is made possible by the phenomenology of language. Unlike Dilthey, who largely reserved the metaphysical impulse to abstract philosophical systems, we have extended it to everyday life as well. And unlike Wittgenstein, who believed that the bewitchment of intelligence by language could be overcome by good philosophizing, we contend that such bewitchment is an indelible feature of the never-ending struggle against the tragedy of finitude.

7

EXPERIENCING SELFHOOD IS NOT "A SELF"

> The contemporary analysis of human existence fills us all with a sense of fragility, with the power of dark instincts, with the suffering caused by mysteries and illusions, and with the finitude shown by all that is living, even where the highest creations of communal life arise from it.
>
> (Wilhelm Dilthey, 1910, p. 172)

The metaphysical impulse

The first Western philosopher to examine systematically the relationship between the tragedy of human finitude and the ubiquity of metaphysical illusion was Wilhelm Dilthey (1910). As reconstructed by de Mul (2004), Dilthey's life's work can be seen as an effort to replace the Kantian *a priori*—the timeless forms of perception and categories of cognition through which the world becomes intelligible to us—with "life categories" that are historically contingent and constituted over the course of a living historical process. There is a tragic dimension to Dilthey's historical consciousness, in that it brings out the "tragic contradiction between the philosophical desire for universal validity [the metaphysical impulse] and the realization of the fundamental finitude of every attempt to satisfy that desire" (de Mul, 2004, p. 154). Dilthey's recognition of this tragic contradiction leads him to elaborate a hermeneutic phenomenology of metaphysics.

Dilthey's historical reconstruction of the development of metaphysics aims at no less than its "euthanasia." Although he holds that metaphysical desire is inherent to human nature, what he seeks to unmask are the illusions that this ubiquitous desire creates. Metaphysical illusion, according to Dilthey, transforms historically-contingent nexuses of intelligibility—worldviews, as he eventually calls them—into timeless forms of reality. Anticipating Heidegger (1927), Dilthey holds that every worldview is grounded in a mood regarding the tragic realization of the finitude of life. The metaphysicalization of worldviews transforms the unbearable fragility and transience of all things human into an enduring, permanent, changeless reality, an illusory world of eternal truths. The metaphysical impulse was grasped by both Dilthey and Heidegger as a relentless tendency to transform the experience of the real into a reified vision of the REALLY real.

The tragic and the metaphysical in psychoanalytic theory

George Klein (1976) claims that Freud's psychoanalytic theory actually amalgamates two theories—a metapsychology and a clinical theory—deriving from two different universes of discourse. Metapsychology deals with the material substrate of experience and is couched in the natural science framework of impersonal structures, forces, and energies.

Clinical theory, by contrast, deals with intentionality and the unconscious meanings of personal experience, seen from the perspective of the individual's unique life history.

Clinical psychoanalysis asks "why" questions and seeks answers in terms of personal reasons, purposes, and individual meanings. Metapsychology asks "how" questions and seeks answers in terms of the non-experiential realm of impersonal mechanisms and causes. Klein sought to disentangle metapsychological and clinical concepts, retaining only the latter as the legitimate content of psychoanalytic theory. For Klein, the essential psychoanalytic enterprise involves the reading of disclaimed intentionality and the unlocking of unconscious meanings from a person's experience, a task for which the concepts of the clinical theory, purged of metapsychological contaminants, are uniquely suited. Klein's proposals for a radical "theorectomy" for psychoanalysis have significantly influenced such contemporary thinkers as Merton Gill, Roy Schafer, and those, including ourselves, who have sought to rethink psychoanalysis as a form of phenomenological inquiry.

Expanding on Klein's distinction, we might characterize psychoanalytic clinical theory as emotional phenomenology and psychoanalytic metapsychology as a form of metaphysics, in that it postulates ultimate realities and universal truths. We think this division is characteristic of all the major psychoanalytic theories—they are mixtures of emotional phenomenology and metaphysics. Emotional phenomenology embodies the tragic, in that emotional experiencing is finite, transient, context-dependent, ever-changing, and decaying. Metapsychology evades the tragic by means of metaphysical illusion. Phenomenology/metapsychology is a trauma-driven binary insofar as finite human existing, stripped of sheltering illusions, is inherently traumatizing (Stolorow, 2011).

Let us turn to the dialectic of the tragic and the metaphysical as it shows up in Heinz Kohut's (1977) psychoanalytic psychology of the self. Kohut's prodigious contributions to clinical psychoanalysis pertained to a dimension of emotional phenomenology—the experiencing (note the verb) of a sense of selfhood. The theoretical language of self psychology, with its noun, "the self," reifies the experiencing of selfhood and transforms it into a metaphysical entity with thing-like properties. "A self" has two poles, joined by a tension arc. It can be cohesive or fragmented. It can be enfeebled, but, in psychoanalysis, it can be rehabilitated. Sometimes it even has the characteristics of a human agent, as when it seeks selfobjects (more entities) or, when fragmented, it somehow performs actions to restore its cohesion.

What is wrong with this reifying theoretical language and why does it matter clinically? To us, Kohut's (1971, 1977) lasting and most important contribution to psychoanalytic clinical theory was his recognition that the experiencing of selfhood is always constituted, both developmentally and in psychoanalytic treatment, in a context of emotional interrelatedness. The experiencing of selfhood, he realized, or of its collapse, is context-embedded through and through.

What does theoretical talk of "the self" do to Kohut's hard-won clinical contextualizations? In effect, it undoes them! "A self" as a metaphysical entity with thing-like properties is ontologically (i.e., in its being or intelligibility) decontextualized, much as the Cartesian mind, a "thinking thing," was ontologically isolated from its world. A thing remains the self-same thing that it is whether it is with you or with one of us. Reifying and transforming the experiencing of selfhood into an entity, "a self" with an "intrinsic . . . nuclear program" (Kohut, 1984, p. 42) or "basic design" (p. 160), strips such experiencing of its exquisite context-sensitivity and context-dependence—the very context-embeddedness that it was Kohut's great contribution to have articulated!

Perhaps such stripping is the very purpose served by these substantializing objectifications. Might they not serve, through metaphysical illusion, to evade a dimension of the tragic familiar to anyone who has experienced an emotional-world-shattering loss—the tragic dimension of human existence that we have previously characterized as "the unbearable embeddedness of being" (Stolorow and Atwood, 1992, p. 22)? (Kohut himself experienced at least two world-shattering discontinuities in the course of his development—one brought about by the impact on his family life of World War I and his father's enlistment and becoming a prisoner of war during Heinz's infancy, and the other resulting from the destruction of his world by the Nazis when he was a medical student in Vienna (Strozier, 2001).) The objectification of the experiencing of selfhood serves to render stable and solid a sense of personal identity otherwise subject to discontinuity, uncertainty, and fragmentation. A phenomenological-contextualist viewpoint, by contrast, embraces the unbearable vulnerability and context-dependence of human existence.

Kohut (1977) described man, as seen through the lens of his psychology of the self, as a "Tragic Man [who] seeks to express the pattern of his nuclear self [but whose] failures overshadow his successes" (p. 133). It is our view that Kohut's concept of tragic man misses the tragedy residing at the heart of human existence as such, prior to any formation of nuclear ambitions and ideals—namely, the tragedy of human finitude itself and the inevitability of decay, death, and loss.

How metaphysical language bewitches intelligence

Just how is the illusory transformation of the experiencing of selfhood into a metaphysical entity accomplished? Wittgenstein's account, which we discussed in the previous chapter, of how language bewitches one's intelligence, provides a cogent explanation of how such a transformation can occur. The meaning of a word is thought to be found in a projected picture, and the picture, in turn, is imagined to correspond to an ultimately real thing-in-itself. The word *self*, for example, becomes transformed into a metaphysical entity, "a self." In place of the "muddied" view given by experiential selfhood—finite, contingent, unstable, and transient, disorganizing and reorganizing in changing relational contexts—one can imagine the clear outlines of a stable bipolar structure that will endure for generations, much like the tripartite structure of Freudian metapsychology. Metaphysical illusion replaces the tragic finitude and transience of human existence with a God's-eye picture of an irreducibly absolute and eternally changeless reality.

Dialogue

GEA: These two chapters (6 and 7) fit together very beautifully, Bob, in that the reification of the concept of "the self" may be regarded as a special case of the metaphysicalization of linguistic terms in general.

RDS: Yes, and this transformation of our words and concepts, as we have argued, serves to evade the ever-shifting context-dependence of the meanings of our words and provides for our discourse a reassuring illusion of stability, substantiality, and coherence.

GEA: It strikes me that our thoughts here represent the latest and most extreme development in a theme that has preoccupied us since the mid 1970s—namely, the critique of metapsychology. In our first book, *Faces in a Cloud* (Stolorow and Atwood, 1979), we showed how great systems of personality theory were structured around reified and universalized images of core human experiences, images reflecting and symbolizing the personal solutions the theorists had found to their own most central issues and conflicts. Metapsychology, we noted in our book, closely resembles metaphysics in philosophy in that both are preoccupied with absolutes and universals. Eventually, we saw that metapsychology is a form of metaphysics.

RDS: At first, we imagined the possibility of a metapsychology-free science of human experience dispensing with such universalizing reifications, one that would address personal subjective worlds in all their richness and diversity. Gradually, however, we have recognized that the dream of breaking free of metapsychology is not to be fulfilled, because theoretical formulations in our field, including our own, always and inevitably display the presence of a metaphysical impulse.

GEA: And here we are extending this idea to the sphere of the everyday life of human beings in general. It is not just the great theorists in our discipline who are metaphysicians; so are we all in the way we regard our most fundamental communications with one another.

RDS: Yes George, we have realized, following Dilthey, that we all engage in forms of metaphysical evasion of the traumas of human finitude and transience.

GEA: The evasion of finitude and transience is becoming a universal in our thinking, a part of the shared experience of the human condition from which no one is exempt. Would it then be correct to say that the metaphysical impulse is itself a part of our own metaphysics?

RDS: I think that would depend on exactly how this impulse is conceptualized—if the emphasis is placed on metaphysics as an *enduring and essential* feature of human experience, then we are positing the existence of a theme of human life that is invariably, universally present. There is a paradox here.

GEA: I am reminded of something I ran across in a study of Sartre's (1943) *Being and Nothingness*, years ago (Atwood, 1983). What Sartre described as "being-for-itself," human consciousness, is pictured in his philosophy as forever longing to possess the definition and solidity of "being-in-itself," which is the realm of materially objective things. Things have a permanence and a determinate nature, consciousness does not. But being-for-itself is always seeking that absent constancy, that reassuring solidity, and identifies itself with objects and denies its own nothingness. A kind of dialectic appears in his portrait of our subjective life, a back-and-forth movement between affirming our limitless freedom and denying it in acts of so-called bad faith. This oscillation turns out to be *the permanent structure of human existence and is Sartre's metaphysics.*

RDS: Wouldn't it be our answer to this paradox that we do not propose the metaphysical impulse—the need to evade finitude and transience—as the universally central organizing theme of the human condition? It is instead in our understanding just one theme among an indefinitely large collection of others that may organize personal subjective worlds. Metaphysics, by contrast, typically grounds its generalizations in entities subsisting independently of human experience—in an *everlasting, immutable in-itself.*

GEA: Something further is coming up for me in relation to the ideas developed in this chapter: a question about our understanding of the nature of language itself. What is language? What "picture" springs to mind when this word is spoken? And does that picture turn into a metaphysical absolute, freezing our thinking about the symbols we are using to express our thoughts and communicate with each other?

RDS: Maybe it would be interesting to relate this question to the ideas of Charles Taylor (2016), whose book *The Language Animal* we recently read together. Two broad views of the nature of language—two ways of understanding what language is—are described by Taylor. One of these, deriving from rationalism and British empiricism, he describes as "enframing" or "designative"—the role of language is to signify objects in a world already fully formed. The other, coming down to us from German Romanticism, he characterizes as "constitutive," in which language actually shapes the world it purports to describe. Would you want to somehow connect Taylor's analysis to Wittgenstein's reflections, George?

GEA: Yes, I would. The so-called enframing perspective seeks to account for language within a framework that is not itself linguistic. The accounts given are atomistic and reductive. The constitutive view, in contrast, leads to a holistic interpretation of language, one recognizing that language confers meaning upon the world we experience and could never be explained in entirely non-linguistic terms.

Here is what I think. The reductive-atomistic view, enframing and explaining away language in terms of factors and processes operating independently of it, is actually itself a Wittgensteinian "picturing" of language's essence, and leads to a metaphysicalization from which there can be no recovery. Language is reduced to something other than itself, becomes just one capacity among many others, a learned group of responses, a skill-set pressed into service to facilitate human communication. It thereby loses its mystery and its generative power as the precondition for thinking and questioning in general. This would be the constitutive perspective, from which language is seen as creating the irreducible possibility of human thought itself. You and I, Bob, embrace a radically constitutive view.

RDS: Charles Taylor, in his book on language, seems for the most part in favor of the constitutive perspective, but finds a place for the enframing or designative perspective in scientific discourse. Such a compromise leaves the scientism of our current era unchallenged. Scientism embodies a hidden metaphysics in which the objects designated, not constituted, by scientific language are elevated to the status of grounding metaphysical entities.

GEA: Adopting a wholeheartedly constitutive approach, language ceases to be any sort of defined "thing" at all. Language becomes instead a universal condition intrinsic to our shared way of life, its core resting in the symbolic function. The subjective world of a human being is uniquely, first and foremost, a *symbolic* world, a world that is suffused with language from the outset.

8

PHENOMENOLOGY AND METAPHYSICAL REALISM

Robert D. Stolorow

This chapter extends the earlier chapter co-written with George Atwood in which we joined Wilhelm Dilthey's conception of the metaphysical impulse as a flight from the tragedy of human finitude with Ludwig Wittgenstein's understanding of how language bewitches intelligence. We contended that there are features of the phenomenology of language identified by Wittgenstein—in particular, the projection of reified pictures as the meaning of words—that play a constitutive and pervasive role in the creation of metaphysical illusion. Unlike Dilthey, who largely reserved the metaphysical impulse to abstract philosophical systems, we extended it to everyday life as well. And, unlike Wittgenstein, who believed that the bewitchment of intelligence by language could be overcome by good philosophizing, we argued that such bewitchment is an indelible feature of the never-ending struggle against the traumatizing impact of finitude.

Ricoeur (1977) claimed, "Philosophical pleading for subjectivity"—that is, phenomenology—"is becoming the citizen's only recourse against the tyrant" (p. 155). Our account of the genesis of metaphysical illusion provides a means of unpacking Ricoeur's claim. Typically, tyranny is supported by some form of totalitarian ideology, and totalitarian ideology, in turn, is ordinarily rooted in a framework of metaphysical illusion or what is oxymoronically characterized as *metaphysical realism*.

In her study of totalitarianism, Hannah Arendt (1951) provided a cogent analysis of the essence of political ideology. Such "isms," she said, claim to explain all historical happenings by deducing them from a single self-evident idea or premise–for example, that history "progresses" through the elimination of inferior races (Nazism) or decadent classes (communism). Once established, these ironclad logical systems become, like paranoid delusions, immune to the impact of actual experience. Further, they readily devolve into systems of genocidal terror, as they give warrant to the unbridled liquidation of anyone or anything believed to impede the historical process.

An all-too-common form of totalitarian ideology is found in the rhetoric of evil. The seeds of the rhetoric of evil can be found in the ancient religious ideology, originating in Persia and pervasive in contemporary religious fundamentalism, known as *Manichaeism*—the idea that the movement of history is explained by an eternal struggle between the metaphysical forces of good and of evil. In the rhetoric of evil, Manichaeism is harnessed for political purposes—one's own group is claimed to embody the forces of good, and the opposing group the forces of evil. Through such attributions, which are inherently nationalistic or ethnocentric, one's political aims are justified as being in the service of the good.

What Ricoeur calls *philosophical pleading for subjectivity* I want to call *phenomenology*. As George Atwood and I have shown in an earlier chapter, the phenomenological study of language can be effective in deconstructing metaphysical illusions, including those that support totalitarian ideologies. Heidegger (1927), for example, carries out his phenomenological investigation of the meaning of Being in conjunction with a "destruction" (p. 44) of traditional ontological concepts in which Being is regarded as some sort of metaphysical entity.

As distinct from a metaphysical essence that inheres in entities themselves, Heidegger conceives of the Being of entities in terms of how they are intelligible or understandable *to us* as the entities they are. The Being of entities thus depends on human understanding—the "clearing" that lights up their intelligibility. Heidegger argues that, because an unarticulated, pre-philosophical understanding of our own Being is constitutive of our kind of Being, we humans can investigate our own kind of Being by investigating our understanding (and lack of understanding) of that Being. Accordingly, it follows that his investigative method is to be a phenomenological one, aimed at *illuminating the fundamental structures of our understanding of our Being*: "*Only as phenomenology, is ontology possible*" (p. 60). In this formulation, the positing of metaphysical entities and essences gives way to a phenomenological investigation and illumination of how entities, including especially we ourselves, are intelligible.

Soon after the publication of *Being and Time*, Heidegger turned his attention from the Being of entities to *Being as such*, a phrase that seems to point in a metaphysical direction. Indeed, inspired by the poet Holderlin as his guide to a spiritual awakening, he characterizes Being as such as a divine force or energy, "sent" to the properly receptive human being (Heidegger 1968). In recent years, a debate has been taking place among members of the Heidegger Circle as to whether the later Heidegger remained dedicated to phenomenological inquiry or turned instead to a form of metaphysical realism. The crux of the debate concerns the question of whether Being as such remains dependent on the human being (phenomenology) or is independent of the human beings who experience it (metaphysical realism). Over the years, proponents of both sides of the debate have marshaled plausible support from Heidegger's original texts. Perhaps we can conclude that this debate reflects a conflict within Heidegger himself over these two opposing conceptions, a conflict rooted in his own experiential world.

There is one context, however, in which Heidegger's pivot toward metaphysical realism is undeniable—namely, his embrace of Nazi ideology. Heidegger's version of Nazism reflected his own dream of Being, whereby he seemed to experience the Nazi takeover of Germany as an upsurge of Being itself, bursting forth in historical reality. He envisioned a "second beginning" in the history of Being (the first occurring in ancient Greece) in which he himself would be a spiritual leader. As seen in the case of Heidegger's "turn" toward Being as such, forms of metaphysical realism can underpin both a destructive ideology and an inspiring spirituality.

Collective trauma and resurrective ideology

Returning to the claim made by Ricoeur, how can phenomenology help emancipate people from such metaphysical illusions? In a chapter co-written with George Atwood and Donna Orange (Stolorow, 2011, Chapter 9), we argued that, for Heidegger, Nazism was an example of what we called *resurrective ideology*, which served to restore a sense of agentic selfhood that had been dismantled by a series of devastating traumatic occurrences. A similar restorative purpose can be served on a socio-political scale by destructive ideologies that take form in the wake of collective trauma—witness, for example, the rise of Manichean rhetoric in the aftermath of the terrorist attack on the World Trade Center on September 11, 2001 (Stolorow, 2009), a devastating collective trauma that inflicted "a rip in the fabric" (Lear, 2006, p. 65) of the American psyche.

In horrifyingly demonstrating that even America can be assaulted on its native soil, the attack of 9/11 shattered our collective illusions of safety, inviolability, and grandiose invincibility, illusions that had long been mainstays of the American historical identity. In the wake of such shattering, Americans became much more susceptible to resurrective ideologies that promised to restore the grandiose illusions that have been lost. It was in this context of collective trauma and resurrective ideology that Americans fell prey to the abuses of power of the Bush administration. Following 9/11, Bush et al. did not merely go after Al Qaeda. Fueling and exploiting the dread of retraumatization, they declared war on global terrorism and drew America into a grandiose, holy crusade that enabled Americans to feel delivered from trauma and "to bathe themselves collectively in the belief that we are that blessed City on a Hill called upon by the Lord to rid the world of evil" (Davis, 2006, p. xiv). Bush essentially said to us:

> You have not been devastated and crushed. You are not exposed as excruciatingly vulnerable human beings, just as vulnerable to assault, destruction, death, and loss, as are all other people around the world. You are still great and powerful, godlike, and together we will bring our way of life to every nation on earth.

Tragically, every effort to actualize such ideological illusions inflicts collective trauma on those whom we attack, and they respond with an intensification of their resurrective ideologies. It is this dialectic of traumatic collapse and ideological resurrection that fuels the lamentable, endlessly recurring cycle of atrocity and counteratrocity that has been so characteristic of human history. Davis (2006) suggests that to learn from history we must be able to live in experiences of collective trauma rather than grandiosely evade them. I would add with regard to the trauma of 9/11 that we must be able to grieve—grieve not only for the people who were killed but also for the illusions and innocence we have lost. How can this be done?

An alternative: Siblings in the same darkness

In search of an alternative to resurrective ideology, I return to the theme of emotional trauma's context-embeddedness and, especially, to the claim that emotional trauma can gradually become integrated when it finds a relational home in which it can be held. What makes the finding of such a relational home possible?

I have contended (Stolorow, 2007) that, just as finitude and vulnerability to death and loss are fundamental to our existential constitution, so too is it constitutive of our existence that we meet each other as "brothers and sisters in the same dark night" (Vogel, 1994, p. 97), deeply connected with one another in virtue of our common finitude. Thus, although the possibility of emotional trauma is ever present, so too is the possibility of forming bonds of deep emotional attunement within which devastating emotional pain can be held, rendered more tolerable, and, hopefully, eventually integrated. Our existential kinship-in-the-same-darkness is the condition for the possibility both of the profound contextuality of emotional trauma and of the mutative power of human understanding.

Imagine a society in which the obligation to provide a relational home for the emotional pain that is inherent to the traumatizing impact of our finitude has become a shared ethical principle. In such a society, human beings would be much more capable of living in their existential vulnerability, anxiety, and grief, rather than having to revert to the defensive, destructive evasions of them that I have been discussing. In such a societal context, a new form of identity would become possible, based on owning rather than covering up our existential vulnerability. Vulnerability that finds a hospitable relational home could be seamlessly and constitutively integrated into whom we experience ourselves as being. A new form of human solidarity would also become possible rooted not in shared resurrective grandiosity but in shared recognition and respect for our common human finitude. If we can help one another bear the darkness rather than evade it, perhaps one day we will be able to see the light.

How can phenomenological inquiry loosen the grip of restorative ideological illusions? It can do so by helping people understand and dwell in the traumas—individual or collective—that underpin them, thereby providing the emotional devastation with a dialogical home in which it can be held and better borne (Stolorow, 2016), rendering the evasive resurrective ideological illusions less necessary. If, as Braver (2012) quips, "Phenomenology lets metaphysicians heal themselves" (p. 31), perhaps it can do something similar for ideologues.

Dialogue

GEA: In reading over your thoughts on metaphysical realism and the concept of evil, my own musings on the phenomenology of evil came to mind. One can look at evil not as a thing, metaphysical or otherwise, but as an experience of which every human being is capable. What is the nature of the experience of evil? This would be our sense that something or someone before us is an implacable, determined threat to the existence of all we hold precious. It is the experience of absolute malevolence, where one becomes aware that a person or group is absolutely dedicated to the destruction of what we most deeply love and cherish—ourselves, our children, our faith, our very worlds as ours to inhabit. An individual is catapulted into the experience of being confronted by evil when he or she perceives the presence of that threat.

RDS: Adopting a phenomenological perspective focusing on evil invites a study of the specific contexts in which evil as an experience appears and is magnified. Hannah Arendt, for example, formulated her view of "radical evil"—a stripping of human beings of that which makes them distinctively human—in the context of the dehumanizing atrocities of the Holocaust.

GEA: Evil, phenomenologically considered, is something that is felt or sensed, and is not to be regarded as an entity having objective existence. We see a demon before us, and we can ask about the conditions and contexts within which such a perception appears. This is an empirical–phenomenological question, to be answered by studying examples of the experience in concrete human lives. Bruce Wilshire (2004), my dear friend in philosophy at Rutgers, wrote a book on genocide—entitled *Get 'Em All, Kill 'Em!*—in which he discussed this sort of thing, arguing that genocide occurs when one group begins to experience another group as a dire threat to what he calls the "world-experienced"—i.e., the familiar cultural universe in which members of the former group live. His book is a contribution to the phenomenology of evil, and to the understanding of the consequences that tend to flow from this experience. When people feel confronted by evil, they do desperate, terrible things to avert it, obliterate it, and thereby remove the threat to the "world-experienced."

RDS: An attack against a person or a group perceived as evil may itself create a context inducing a corresponding experience of evil in a destructive synchrony and reciprocity.

GEA: Yes. A few years ago, my son Christopher, then 15 years old, and I formulated a thought that is relevant to this discussion. We referred to the Satanic, rather than to evil, but it reduces to the same thing: "*The idea that one has identified the Satanic is itself the Satanic.*"

RDS: I see that this thought is self-referential and paradoxical, in that in identifying the Satanic, it itself becomes an instance *of* the Satanic.

GEA: The thinking here is that, when one is confronted with evil, as an experience, the only response that makes any sense, the ONLY thing one can do, is to devote the totality of one's energies to destroying it. It will destroy you, so destroy it first! My son's and my little thought invites its own destruction. One responds to those who appear, in our subjectivity, to embody evil by rising up against them, threatening and attacking them, tending inevitably to produce in their experience a sense that one is oneself the embodiment of evil. A counterattack then occurs, and the human beings involved fall into a death spiral. Absolute conviction on the one side provokes absolute counter-conviction on the other, and there is nothing that can stop the conflict except for the obliteration of one or both sides. My son and I intended our thought as a kind of warning to stay away from the concept of evil, of the Satanic, because as soon as one applies it, a sequence of events as described above is set in motion. Think of George Bush's use of the phrase, "Axis of Evil," deadly words heard by those to whom they were directed, words perceived to have been spoken by The Great Satan. The idea of evil as something metaphysically real should be banned from political discourse, as well as from psychology. But we need to understand it as an experience that some of us have, and of which all of us are capable. Evil in this latter, phenomenological sense is therefore to be viewed as a special kind of psychological catastrophe, one that belongs to that extreme range of subjective events involving the threat of personal annihilation.

RDS: Metaphysical realism in general, as we understand it, arises out of the suffering of finitude, the unbearable embeddedness of being in the transitory, ever-shifting contexts of our experience of ourselves and our worlds. Given the omnipresence of this realism, perhaps we should ask whether traces of such thinking appear again in our own philosophical and psychological formulations.

GEA: Yes, is the concept of the metaphysical impulse itself metaphysical? If we were to say that there is a universal impulse to discover or uncover the unmoved mover, the solid ground of all grounds, the ultimate World Turtle on which rests the infinite series of turtles all the way down, does this formulation itself provide such a foundation and thereby constitute an example of itself?

RDS: The idea of the metaphysical impulse is not pictured as something solidly tangible and physical, but it does at least lean in the direction of ubiquity. So, we can ask: is the theory of the metaphysical impulse on the way to becoming our metapsychology? Our answer to this question is to look toward the constitutive contexts belonging to this idea and its universalization. Why would we need to embrace this concept in the first place, and why would we need to expose or establish its ubiquity in human life?

GEA: If we posit the existence of a metaphysical impulse in the heart of human nature, we arrive at a changeless core of our existence—the very need to find a changeless core. It is somewhat like the paradox of Buddhism, which offers the idea that there is one and only one constant of human existence—that constant is nothing other than Change. We have noticed that Buddhists often laugh and laugh when this statement is made, peals of silvery laughter, and they are so pleased in its contemplation. It seems to liberate them from helpless entrapment in things that cannot be controlled or modified, from all victimizing circumstances; but it also gives them a constant to hang on to, to embrace in a metaphysical thrill that simultaneously affirms and denies itself. Are we also made to laugh at our ideas, and are we similarly thrilled?

RDS: I'm not laughing and I am not thrilled, George, but I think I see a source of the problem you are wrestling with. It is implicit in the language you are using—"changeless core" located "in the heart of human nature"—phrases that point to metaphysical entities and essences. But an experience, even the experience of a metaphysical impulse, cannot be *both* a metaphysical entity or essence, which by definition would make it context-independent, *and* constituted contextually, as we are claiming of the metaphysical impulse.

What are the myriad constitutive contexts of our gravitation toward the idea of the metaphysical impulse? Perhaps, if we can expose metaphysical illusion everywhere we see it, we can bring about a world of siblings in the same darkness, and we can all dwell together in the tragedy of human finitude and its many manifestations—illness, frailty, failure, death, traumatic loss, etc. The only solution I can see to the suffering of finitude, far from a perfect one, is for us to soften its impact through the bonds of love we establish with one another.

9

PHENOMENOLOGICAL CONTEXTUALISM AND THE FINITUDE OF KNOWING

Robert D. Stolorow

> There is *only* a perspective seeing, *only* a perspective "knowing"; and the *more* affects we allow to speak about one thing, the *more* eyes, different eyes, we can use to observe one thing, the more complete will our "concept" of this thing, our "objectivity," be.
>
> (Friedrich Nietzsche, 1887, p. 555)

> We cannot look around our own corner. . . . We are . . . far from the ridiculous immodesty that would be involved in decreeing from our corner that perspectives are permitted only from this corner.
>
> (Friedrich Nietzsche, 1882, p. 374)

In this chapter, I want to show that the two foregoing quotations from Nietzsche provide the basis for an epistemic stance appropriate to *the finitude of knowing*.

In the first quotation, Nietzsche (1887) establishes himself as a consummate phenomenologist, pointing to the prereflective structures—i.e., the perspectives— that shape our perceptions and understandings. Such structures form what Heidegger (1927), refuting his teacher Husserl's claims about "presuppositionless inquiry," calls "the forestructure of understanding and the as-structure of interpretation" (p.192). Just as Nietzsche's (1882) madman declared that God is dead, so too has the God's-eye view become extinct. Expressed in another metaphor, there is no "immaculate perception" (Nietzsche, 1892, p. 233). Because of the perspectival nature of all perception and understanding, Nietzsche is claiming, truth can only be dialogic, taking form in the interplay among many eyes and many interpreters. As Braver (2007) aptly puts it, Nietzsche provides "a non-metaphysical way to read [the perception of] chaos as the idea that the world is indefinitely pliable to various interpretations . . ." (p.158).

In the second quotation, closely related to the first, Nietzsche (1882) establishes himself as an equally consummate contextualist, claiming that our interpretive perspective is always embedded in the corner of the world—the context—from which our seeing and understanding are constituted. And, he contends, there is no privileged corner that reigns supreme above all others. Thus, Nietzsche's phenomenological contextualism of necessity gives rise to an attitude of epistemic humility.[1]

Gadamer, who was Heidegger's student, makes the surprising claim that "the true predecessor of Heidegger was neither Dilthey nor Husserl, . . . but rather *Nietzsche*" (Gadamer, 1975, p. 257, italics in original). The claim is quite plausible with regard to at least one aspect of Heidegger's thought—namely, his phenomenological-contextualist perspective—for which Nietzsche's perspectivism was a forerunner and which Gadamer developed even further.

Axiomatic for Gadamer (1975) is the proposition that all understanding involves interpretation. Interpretation, in turn, can only be from a perspective embedded in the historical matrix of the interpreter's own traditions. Understanding, therefore, is always from a perspective whose horizons are delimited by the historicity of the interpreter's preconceptions, by the fabric of "fore-meanings" that Gadamer calls *prejudice*. Gadamer illustrates his hermeneutical philosophy by applying it to the anthropological problem of attempting to understand an alien culture in which the forms of social life, the horizons of experience, are incommensurable with those of the investigator. He also applies it to the phenomenon of intersubjective conversation—"a process of coming to an understanding" (p. 385) with another person—a process that has enormous relevance for psychoanalysis.

The "hermeneutic attitude," which, according to Gadamer, maximizes the possibility of expanded understanding within a conversation, consists in two components. First, each participant recognizes that his/her understanding is conditioned and delimited by his/her prejudices. These prejudices cannot be expunged, but their limiting impact on understanding can be recognized and acknowledged. Second, and following from the first, there is recognition of the full value of the alien, as "each person opens himself/herself to the other [and] truly accepts his/her point of view as valid" (p. 385). An expansion of understanding takes place through a "fusion of horizons" (p. 388), in which each perspective becomes enlarged by features of the other's. Thus, "in genuine dialogue, something emerges that is contained in neither of the partners by himself/herself" (p. 462). In Gadamer's phenomenological-contextualist vision, truth and understanding are dialogic, constituted in the interplay of differently organized worlds of experience.

It will probably come as no surprise that, like the philosophies discussed so far, *intersubjective-systems theory*, my collaborators' and my (Stolorow, Atwood, and Orange, 2002) post-Cartesian psychoanalytic framework, is also a phenomenological-contextualist perspective. It is phenomenological in that it investigates and illuminates worlds of emotional experience and the structures that organize them. It is contextualist in that it holds that such structures take form, both developmentally and in the psychoanalytic situation, in constitutive intersubjective contexts. Developmentally, recurring patterns of intersubjective transaction within the developmental system give rise to principles (thematic patterns, meaning-structures, as-structures, prejudices, etc.) that unconsciously organize subsequent emotional and relational experiences. As I have said in an earlier chapter, such organizing principles are unconscious, not in the sense of being repressed but in being prereflective; they ordinarily do not enter the domain of reflective self-awareness. These intersubjectively-derived, prereflective organizing principles are the basic building blocks of personality development, and their totality constitutes a person's character. They show up in the psychoanalytic situation in the form of transference, which intersubjective-systems theory conceptualizes as unconscious organizing activity. The patient's transference experience is co-constituted by the patient's prereflective organizing principles and whatever is coming from the analyst that is lending itself to being organized by them. A parallel statement can be made about the analyst's transference. The psychological field formed by the interplay of the patient's transference and the analyst's transference is an example of what we call an *intersubjective system*—a system that can attain a staggering degree of complexity.

We have found it useful clinically to distinguish two broad dimensions of transference or two broad classes of organizing principles. In one, the *developmental dimension*, the patient longs for the analyst to be a source of development-enhancing emotional experiences that were aborted, lost, or missing during the formative years. In the other, the *repetitive dimension*, the patient anticipates, fears, or experiences with the analyst a repetition of early emotional trauma. Each of these broad dimensions can be divided further into multiple sub-dimensions deriving from different developmental eras and experiences with different caregivers. The various dimensions shift between the background and foreground of the patient's emotional experience, often quite rapidly and unpredictably, depending on the meanings of activities or qualities of the analyst. Tracking these figure-ground shifts as they occur in response to happenings within the intersubjective field can bring intelligibility to a therapeutic situation otherwise experienced as chaotic and incomprehensible.

As if this weren't complex enough, however, the same description also applies to the analyst's transference—multiple dimensions oscillating between the background and foreground of the analyst's experience depending on the meanings for the analyst of activities or qualities of the patient. We have a picture, then, of a complex system formed by two multidimensional, fluidly oscillating emotional worlds interacting with and mutually influencing one another, all in response to the meanings of goings-on within the intersubjective field. As I like to say, anyone looking for Cartesian clarity and apodictic certainty here has come to the wrong place!

On a clinical note, especially vexing for many people is the limitedness of our ability to know the outcomes of our decision-making in advance. Being troubled about this limitation can be particular acute for someone who grew up feeling alone and unprotected in childhood situations of emotional trauma and who turned to his or her own mental activity as the only source of protectedness and safety. Covering every base in advance is of paramount importance for such a person, and the limited ability to do so is anathema to him or her, resulting in unbearable anxiety and a propensity for obsessional rumination, doubt, and indecision. In a therapeutic situation, a person tormented by this legacy of emotional trauma needs to find in the therapeutic bond a source of protectedness and safety, along with a relational home—a context of emotional understanding—for the unbearable existential anxiety of uncertainty.

In the old days of classical analysis, it was assumed that a neutral analyst could make objective interpretations of the patient's transference experiences as distortions of a reality that the analyst knew directly. Such epistemic arrogance would be completely out of place in a complex intersubjective system to which the organizing activities of both patient and analyst are contributing. And here we find the enormous value of the hermeneutic attitudes recommended by Nietzsche, Heidegger, and Gadamer. When faced with such complexity, in which one is oneself implicated, an epistemic humility that recognizes and respects the finitude of knowing is essential.

Dialogue

GEA: I like all you have said in the above, Bob, but there is something that troubles me in Nietzsche's so-called perspectivism that you seem not to address or be concerned with. I will try to phrase the issue I am having in the form of a question: what is the nature of the viewpoint or perspective embraced by Nietzsche in making the claim that all interpretations of the meaning of the world we experience are perspectival? Since he is characterizing ALL human interpretations, does his idea implicitly ascribe to himself a God's-eye view of a universal truth?

What bothers me here is a bit like something that also comes up for me in thinking about so-called fallibilism in the pragmatism of Charles Sanders Peirce (1931–1935). This philosopher argued that all our theories, all our beliefs, all our opinions, are fallible and therefore should always be "held lightly." Peirce was in rebellion against dogmatic certainties in all their forms and variations. But what about his belief that we should hold all our beliefs lightly? Did he hold that belief lightly too? The answer is No, he made of it a dogma. I find such inconsistency—such incoherence—troubling.

RDS: George, I completely agree that Nietzsche's formulation of perspectivism (like Peirce's assertion of fallibilism) must also apply reflexively to itself—the claim of perspectivism is itself perspectival. But why must this imply a God's-eye view of truth? Instead, to me it is a call for an epistemic humility that eschews a God's-eye view.

GEA: Nietzsche was a man divided and at odds with himself, and his perspectivism has to reflect this personal disunity. He visualizes all interpretations of the world in which human beings live as expressive of and colored by the particular "corners" of the world that the interpreters occupy. At first blush, such a doctrine appears to lead to a commendable humility, reminding us of our finitude as observers and thinkers. But how is such a perspectival view seeing itself as it surveys the vast territory of viewpoints that are conceivable? Could there be an absolutism hiding in Nietzsche's ideas here, a God's-eye view of the essential, universal nature of interpretation itself, and of the human condition as comprised of arrays of unconsciously entrapping "corners" immodestly assumed by their occupants to be universally valid? Is Nietzsche, in making such an argument, implicitly ascribing to his own intelligence the capacity to transcend the presumed fact that human beings are universally "cornered"?

RDS: If this question is answered in the affirmative, then the idea of a "corner" itself may appear to be operating within the structure of his narrative as a metaphysical absolute. I would add, however, that, while there may be a tendency to reify the metaphor of human experience as made up of "corners," as you say, George, we can resist the metaphysicalization of this idea by explicating its own constitutive contexts. Nietzsche's perspectivism is itself still another perspective, constituted by the "corner(s)" in which his own unique subjectivity was located. As you noted above, Nietzsche's personal world was one of deep conflict and disunity.

GEA: Perhaps there is always a tendency toward metaphysicalization in the development of ideas about human nature and the human condition. Although one can never free oneself from this tendency altogether, one can pursue a radical perspectivism and contextualism that seeks reflective self-awareness as a work perpetually in progress.

RDS: Yes! In an earlier chapter we explored how human beings employ certain features of the phenomenology of language in the creation of reassuring metaphysical illusions that serve to evade the traumatizing impact of dimensions of human finitude. And in an earlier "conversation" (Atwood and Stolorow, 2012) we located the constitutive "corners" of some of our own theoretical ideas in aspects of our respective traumatic histories. I emphasized, for example, that my father was an epistemic tyrant, a *Besserwisser*. When our viewpoints were at odds, his was always the correct and valid one. Although he allowed me to argue with him, sometimes vehemently, he never acknowledged the truth and validity in what my eyes saw. Not surprisingly, I have been on the warpath against such epistemic tyranny in psychoanalysis for more than two decades (see Stolorow, 1997a). I love Nietzsche's perspectivism because of its emancipatory power in leveling the epistemic playing field, so, if he wants to absolutize and universalize it, so be it!

I think I tend to metaphysicalize the concept of a constitutive intersubjective context because, as a metaphysical entity, such a context provides eternal protection against epistemic tyranny. When faced with the pronouncements of a psycho-analytic *Besserwisser*, I can, by invoking the idea of constitutive context, reply,

"Well, it all depends!" (Years ago, a student gave me shirt with this claim written on the front.) I once (only once) tried to amalgamate the idea of an intersubjective system with the scientific paradigm of nonlinear systems theory (Stolorow, 1997b), an amalgamation that required that the idea of context be reified and metaphysicalized. Why didn't you stop me, brother?

What is the contribution of your own history to the disagreement we were having? I suspect it has something to do with traumatic loss and invalidation.

GEA: The difference between us here concerned my sense, not initially shared by you, Bob, that there might be a hidden metaphysical absolute in Nietzsche's discussion of his perspectivism. There is something about a closeted absolute that just drives me crazy, and I find myself wanting to hold it up to the light and expose it as such. Even worse, I was afraid our intersubjective contextualism might have been infected by this hidden metaphysics, as we have both fallen heavily under the influence of Nietzsche's philosophy. The danger to which I am responding is not that there could be metaphysics at work in our ideas; it is that this could be the case without our knowing it!

How does the fear of unidentified, unconscious metaphysical absolutes relate to my unique "corner" in this world? It occurs to me that it does so because of a series of lies I was told in the context of the tragic loss of my mother when I was a boy. I had been raised to believe that mothers are always there for their children; mothers do not die. That was the first lie. Second, when my mother was suddenly hospitalized because of unexplained cranial pain, I was reassured by friends of my family that she would be fine and coming home soon. That was the second lie. Third, when I was informed of her death by the minister of my church, he said I would see her again, but would have to wait until I too was in Heaven. I tried to believe this, but was unable to hold on to the idea that Heaven was real. So that was the third lie. The fourth and final lie was one I told myself. I became my mother once more (just as the 4-year-old Nietzsche became the father he had lost; see Atwood, Stolorow, and Orange, 2011), undoing the shattering loss by identifying with her and adopting a personal identity centering on maternal caregiving. In the process of this identification, the boy I had been receded and seemed almost to disappear.

Each of the lies is a metaphysical deception of a kind, nullifying death's dominion and denying the finality and inevitability of loss, thereby rejecting and invalidating my experience of devastating emotional pain. By assiduously exposing the evasive absolutes that may be hiding in the thought of various philosophers and theorists, including myself and Bob Stolorow, a sense of protection from such deceptions is tenuously achieved. My aversion to closeted metaphysical illusions carries my determination never to be deceived and invalidated in that way again. Never again.

GEA, RDS: An essential idea to which we have been led over the course of our collaboration is that of the intersubjective field, understood as a system of interacting, differently organized subjective worlds. This idea, symbolically mirroring the interactive process between the two of us that brought it into being in the first place, we characterized as having the following personal sources and meanings:

> [This idea] universalizes and eternalizes relatedness itself, undoing the traumatizing impact of events in our lives that disrupted emotionally important connections and led to devastating feelings of abandonment and isolation . . . [T]he specific vision of the intersubjective field as a system of interacting, differently organized subjective worlds enshrines at the heart of our theory the hope for a mode of relatedness in which the obliterations of epistemic tyrannies are neutralized and the distinctive structures of individual worlds are respected and preserved.
>
> (Atwood and Stolorow, 2014, p. 127)

The epistemic humility to which our ideas have led us includes a commitment to explore and understand sheltering metaphysical illusions, wherever they appear, in others' thinking or our own. This attitude, far from providing any sense of solace or any solid ground to stand on, is a crying thing that leaves us raw and bleeding, facing the vulnerability and everlasting uncertainty of finite human existing. It also, however, holds out the promise of an ever-deepening journey of self-reflection.

Note

1 During the period of her collaboration with us, Donna Orange, drawing on the fallibilism advocated by Peirce (1931–1935), made important contributions to the fleshing-out of the attitude of epistemic humility in the clinical situation.

10

WALKING THE TIGHTROPE OF EMOTIONAL DWELLING

This essay seeks to characterize an active, relationally engaged form of therapeutic comportment called *emotional dwelling*. Distinctive features of this mode of comportment are identified by contrasting it with corresponding formulations appearing in other theoretical viewpoints, including those of Freud, Ferenczi, Sullivan, and Kohut. Central to emotional dwelling is the therapist's capacity to enter into a patient's reality even while simultaneously holding on to his or her own.

One of us (Stolorow, 2014) recently offered some formulations moving toward this relationally engaged comportment. In dwelling, one does not merely seek to understand the other's emotional world from the other's perspective. One does that, but much more. In dwelling, essential in the pursuit of our discipline's twin goals of ameliorating psychological wounds and exploring human nature and human existence, one leans into the other's experience and participates in it, with the aid of one's own analogous experiences. Here we seek further to identify features of this mode of comportment by contrasting it with other points of view.

Objectification

The antithesis of emotional dwelling is the therapist's attitude of objectification. The most extreme forms of such an attitude are found in crude materialism and behaviorism, wherein the whole concept of the human being as an experiencing subject is abolished. But any way of relating that decontextualizes the experiences being explored objectifies them. Psychiatric diagnosis, for example, ascribes the content and form of the patient's subjective life to particular disorders inhering in an isolated Cartesian mind. Psychoanalytic character types (narcissistic personality, obsessional personality, schizoid personality, etc.), similarly, focus on the patterns of experience and conduct shown by a person seen in isolation from the relational surround. Even the concepts of intersubjective systems theory can be applied in an objectifying manner, as, for instance, when the patterning of subjective life is ascribed to decontextualized "organizing principles" somehow operating within the mind.

Emotional dwelling, in contrast, recognizes the embeddedness of all experience in constitutive intersubjective contexts, including the one created by the act of dwelling itself. We are accordingly led to a view of psychopathology as no longer reducible to an array of discrete mental illnesses, conceived as located somehow within isolated individuals. Instead, the task of diagnosis shifts to the identification of recurrent patterns of disturbance or disequilibrium in complex intersubjective systems. The features of experience and conduct formerly regarded as symptoms of reified psychiatric categorizations or as expressions of decontextualized psychoanalytic character types then become understood as inseparable from the multifaceted relational fields linking the patient to other people, which include the participating presence of the observing clinician.

Evenly hovering attention

Sigmund Freud (1912) famously recommended an attitude for the psychoanalytic clinician of "evenly hovering attention." His idea was that the analyst's sensitivity to the flux of the patient's experiences is maximally enhanced by a kind of floating, open attentiveness, unhampered by conscious preconceptions and purposes. He also suggested that this unguided following of the patient's free associations permits ideas and intuitions to arise out of the analyst's own unconscious mental activity, providing spontaneous insights into otherwise hidden meanings in the clinical material.

Emotional dwelling also aspires to have an openness about its approach to a patient's world, not assuming the presence therein of any particular content or psychological theme. This attitude of openness, however, is not one of suspending preconceptions but rather of searching for areas of intersubjective resonance. The analyst's understanding of the patient's felt situation depends upon an ability to find analogues in his or her own personal universe, emotional scenes, and moments paralleling the experiences being explored. Bringing such territories of correspondence into reflective awareness permits a participation by the analyst in the patient's subjective life as a kindred spirit.

Participant observation

Harry Stack Sullivan (1953) recognized that in psychiatry, as he practiced it, there are no wholly objective facts on which our knowledge can be based. He suggested instead that the scientific data of his discipline are gathered through a process of "participant observation." The instrument of observation is the person of the psychotherapist, who engages with his or her patients and takes note of the phenomena that appear in their reciprocal interaction.

There is a tension in Sullivan's thinking between objectivity and subjectivity, one that importantly distinguishes his understanding from that of emotional dwelling. One sign of this tension appears in the term itself—*participant observation*. It is virtually an oxymoron, the word *observation* connoting detached objectivity, and the word *participant* underlining the highly personal nature of the interaction and the collapse of the distance between the observer and the observed. A second sign of the tension in Sullivan's theory resides in an idea closely associated with that of participant observation—the notion of parataxic distortion. The patient is thought to distort the externally real in order to protect a threatened feeling of security, and Sullivanian therapy, accordingly, has as one of its goals to free the patient from such distortions and thereby enhance the objectivity and accuracy of his or her perceptions of the world. Emotional dwelling, in contrast, is occupied with apprehending subjective truths (Kierkegaard) rather than objective facts. In dwelling, we do not seek to correct the patient's experience and make no assumptions about external reality. While the patient's views frequently differ from those of the analyst, sometimes very dramatically, this difference is endured without judgment being passed as to whose reality is correct. Instead, the analyst searches for the standpoint from which the patient's perceptions and interpretations will show their own inner coherence and validity.

Becoming the patient

In discussing the psychoanalytic therapy of those who have been subjected to an experience of soul murder resulting from traumatic abuse, Sandor Ferenczi (1932) said:

> It is an unavoidable task for the analyst: . . . he will have to repeat with his own hands the act of murder previously perpetrated against the patient. In contrast to the original murderer, however, he is not allowed to deny his guilt.
>
> (p. 58)

He regarded it as essential that the analyst enter fully into the patient's personal world, feeling vicariously its suffering. Rather than approach the psychotherapy process guided by experience-distant theoretical ideas, Ferenczi urged his contemporaries to open themselves up to becoming the patient, viscerally undergoing the traumas that have occurred and that are resurrected in the analytic relationship.

The analyst, in joining the patient's reality and embracing rather than denying his guilt, may be catapulted into unbearable pain. Ferenczi provided little guidance as to how to survive this necessary suffering. One walks on a tightrope, and one can fall on one side or the other. If we fall on the side of complete identification with the patient's reality, we are indicted and condemned for being murderers, corroding our faith in ourselves as therapists. If we fall on the side of protecting our own sense of personal identity—perhaps viewing our patients' experiences of annihilation as results of transference distortions as traditionally understood and our own feelings as products of patients' "projective identifications"—we are exonerated; but the result is to invalidate our patients and repeat their original traumas in full. The answer to the dilemma in an approach based on emotional dwelling is to stay on the rope, holding two differing realities simultaneously–something that is always exceedingly difficult to achieve. In clinical practice, one falls first one way and then the other, and back and forth repeatedly. This difficult oscillation, however, is inevitable along the only pathways to emotional integration that can be found.

Empathic immersion

Traditional notions of therapeutic empathy have been pervaded by the Cartesian doctrine of the isolated mind. This doctrine bifurcates the subjective world of the person into outer and inner regions, reifies and absolutizes the resulting separation between the two, and pictures the mind as a metaphysical entity that takes its place among other objects, a "thinking thing" that has an inside with contents and looks out on an external world from which it is essentially estranged. Within this metaphysical vision, human beings can encounter each other only as thinking subjects, and something like empathic immersion—what Heinz Kohut (1959) famously called vicarious introspection—is required to bridge the ontological gap separating their isolated minds from one another. In a post-Cartesian philosophical world, no such bridging is required, as we are all always already connected with one another in virtue of our common humanity (including our common finitude and existential vulnerability) and our co-disclosive relation to a common world.

Kohut's and others' contention that a therapist's empathic immersions can be neutral and objective is especially saturated with Cartesian assumptions. One isolated mind, the therapist, enters the subjective world of another isolated mind, the patient. With his or her own psychological world virtually left outside, the therapist gazes directly upon the patient's inner experience with pure and preconceptionless eyes. From our vantage point, this doctrine of immaculate perception (Nietzsche) entails a denial of the inherently intersubjective nature of analytic understanding, to which the therapist's subjectivity makes an ongoing, unavertable, and indispensable contribution.

The framework of phenomenological contextualism embraces the hermeneutical axiom that all human thought involves interpretation and that therefore our understanding of anything is always from a perspective shaped and limited by the historicity of our own organizing principles—by the fabric of preconceptions that the philosopher Gadamer (1975) called *prejudice*. The claim that all analytic understanding is interpretive means that there are no decontextualized absolutes and universals, no neutral or objective analysts, no immaculate perceptions, no God's-eye views of anything or anyone—and thus no empathic immersions in another's experiences. This contextualist sensibility keeps our horizons open to multiple, relationally expanded possibilities of meaning. Analytic understanding is thus seen as forming and evolving within a dialogical context.

From our vantage point, therapeutic inquiry is a dialogical process in which each participant, in varying degrees and at different times, engages in reflection upon three interrelated domains—the meanings organizing one's own experience, the meanings organizing the other's experience, and the dynamic intersubjective system constituted by these interacting worlds of meaning. Furthermore, in this dialogical process, each participant (far from entering the other's subjective world and leaving his or her own outside) continually draws on his or her own experiential world in search of analogues for the possible meanings governing the other's experiences. Empathic (introspective) understanding is thus grasped as an emergent property of a dialogical system, rather than as a privileged possession of an isolated mind.

There is something disengaged in the traditional conceptions of therapeutic empathy. Kohut was aware of this, and in his last lecture before he died he characterized empathy as a value-neutral investigative activity that could even be used for malevolent purposes. He suggested that the Nazis' practice of putting sirens on the bombs they dropped on London demonstrated an exquisite empathic understanding of the terror that would be evoked in those on the ground who heard them.

Emotional dwelling contrasts with Kohut's view of empathy. In dwelling, one does not simply seek to understand the other's emotional experiences within the other's frame of reference. One leans into the other's entire emotional situation and participates in it. We have found that this active, engaged, participatory comportment is especially important in the therapeutic approach to emotional trauma. The language that one uses to address another's experience of emotional trauma meets the trauma head-on, articulating the unbearable and the unendurable, saying the unsayable, unmitigated by any efforts to soothe, comfort, encourage, or reassure—such efforts invariably being experienced by the other as a shunning or turning away from his or her traumatized state.

Concluding thoughts

A question may be raised about emotional dwelling as to its limits. How can one dwell with someone's experiences when they differ profoundly from one's own? On what basis can an analyst lean into a patient's subjective situation when the very horizons of possibility (Ratcliffe, 2015) defining the patient's universe depart significantly from the analyst's? Emotional dwelling does not require that the analyst has had identically the same experiences as the patient. It is necessary, however, that thematic analogues be found that will serve to bring their respective worlds into proximity, parallels sharing features in common allowing the analyst to imagine what it is like to be in the patient's situation.

An example appeared in some experiences one of us (George E. Atwood) had during the early stages of his training as a clinical psychologist. A number of the patients he encountered in a psychiatric hospital made statements to the effect that the world was ending or had been destroyed and that they were dead rather than alive. The regular psychiatric staff viewed such statements as delusional, symptoms of a severe mental illness. He did not see them that way—the patients' words seemed to him to be direct expressions of subjective catastrophes that were being felt and lived. This perception in turn made possible in many instances a response allowing the patient to feel understood rather than isolated and pathologized, setting the stage for an eventual therapeutic dialogue. What made this understanding—this emotional dwelling—possible, in view of the fact that he had not himself undergone equivalent experiences of personal annihilation? The answer emerged following long reflection, years after these clinical encounters. Without realizing it explicitly, he had found an analogy in his own life history in a tragic and catastrophic loss that occurred when he was a child. His own early experience of the world ending as he had known it had assisted him in visualizing the experience in his patients of the world ending altogether.

It is our impression that the greatest difficulty analysts have in locating thematic analogues to their patients' experiences resides in areas of their subjective world that have been defensively walled off in order to avert unbearable conflict and pain. An analyst who has disavowed his or her own early experiences of disruption and loss, for example, will be unable to enter the forbidden zone and discover analogies therein to assist in grasping corresponding traumas in the lives of his or her patients. Those who are open to their traumatic histories, in contrast, can draw upon their entire emotional backgrounds as rich resources enabling them to dwell with the troubled souls who turn to them for help. We regard this opening of the analyst's life to the search for thematic analogues to be one of the most important functions of the analyst's own personal analysis.

11

THERE MUST BE BLOOD

The price of emotional dwelling

George E. Atwood

Part 1

I was in the audience a few years ago at a psychoanalytic conference in which a well-known analyst described the "successful treatment" of a man suffering from an obsessive-compulsive neurosis. There were two primary compulsive symptoms that had been present for many years before the patient entered analysis. First, every morning and often at other times during each day, the patient felt it necessary to open every cabinet and pull out every drawer in his home. Then he would close the cabinets and push the drawers back in. Second, he was irresistibly drawn every day to repeatedly bow to the north, the south, the west, and the east—always in that precise sequence.

A seven-year analysis was described, chronicling the developments in a psychotherapeutic relationship conducted on a three-times-a-week basis throughout.

Themes of competition with siblings, toilet training issues in the early years, and struggles with the perfectionism of the parents figured centrally in the account. Dreams symbolically representing these areas of experience were presented and interpreted. The patient was described as always having been on time for his appointments, as having paid his analyst promptly when given a bill, and as having dressed immaculately at every stage. The analysis as a whole seemed to have been a polite conversation between gentlemen, and the symptoms the patient came into treatment with—the cabinets, the drawers, the bowing—were said to have receded over time and vanished. The analyst made the claim that he had "cured" his patient of his neurosis.

I remember a feeling of something burning in my stomach as I listened to this elegant presentation. "Something is not right here," I said to myself. "This is just too perfect."

So, I decided to ask a question and did so: "Where is the blood?" I went on to explain that, although I would never say I had cured anyone of anything, those situations wherein I thought I had provided significant help to someone had always left me covered in blood. This blood came from the missteps, the flashbacks to trauma, the stubborn resistances, the disjunctions between my experiences and those of my patients, from the resurrection and reliving of ancient injuries, from fresh hurts in the present born of my insensitivity and stupidity, from the patients' need to find someone to strike out against.

Throwing caution to the winds, I then offered an alternative interpretation of the case study that had been given. It was my downfall during this difficult afternoon. I said maybe the absence of blood was a sign that nothing fundamental had changed in a life dominated by pleasing the authorities. Perhaps this patient's life was about the theme of compliance, about falling in line, about maintaining the existing order. Was it possible, I continued, that the original symptoms about bowing to all the directions of the compass and the drawers and the cabinets had simply been exchanged for new ones—punctually attending the psychoanalytic sessions and dutifully paying the fees? I even said maybe he was now bowing to his analyst instead of to the north and the south. But is that progress, or is it the same old, same old?

A number of senior analysts in attendance at the talk then rose as one, pronouncing my remarks and questions absurd. They asked the audience as a whole if it could ever make sense to evaluate an analysis by whether or not the analyst is drenched in blood. I felt I had no friends in the room and I had been disgraced.

There is a short sequel to this story. I sat down with the presenter for a few minutes after his talk, and asked about his patient's current situation. He said the patient was very excited that his story was now being told at meetings all around the country. The analyst had secured written permission from the patient to use the account of his treatment in these presentations. I asked him the following question then: "In view of your patient's interest in pleasing you, if he had reservations about your using his story, would he have felt free to refuse you?" The analyst thought for a moment, and then answered, "Maybe not."

I think there needs to be blood.

Part 2

One day, as I was sitting with Bernard Brandchaft, author of *Toward an Emancipatory Psychoanalysis* (Brandchaft, Doctors, and Sorter, 2010), in the backyard of his home in Bel Air, California, he made the following remark to me: "You know, George, in any deep psychotherapy, it's always *mano a mano*." I thought to myself that he was definitely right. Serious psychotherapy is hand-to-hand combat, and there is always blood that is shed.

In the battle that unfolds, it is not the patient that is the adversary. It is a world, one generally rooted in trauma and dominated by the solutions that have been found or constructed long ago. This is the world of a past that has not become past, a history that is lived and relived in an eternal Now. The future in this world, moreover, is not a realm of possibilities, positive and negative, the content of which has yet to be determined; instead, the future is fixed and doomed forever to play out the themes of the past in endless repetitions. The war that commences is between this world and another one, a virtual universe at first—manifest only in faint intimations, being a realm of potentialities, requiring extraordinary and even heroic efforts in order to come into being and be established. The therapist is a representative of this second world, sent from the future to do battle with the reigning powers holding the patient captive. Essential in the drama that unfolds is the validating presence of the therapist as a human being. In his work, particularly in his *Clinical Diary*, which was finally published in 1988, Sándor Ferenczi (1932) described the years of painful, often bloody treatment processes with severely traumatized patients. In an entry in the *Diary* on March 8, 1932, entitled "The analyst as undertaker," Ferenczi's words are:

> I have finally come to realize that it is an unavoidable task for the analyst: Although he may behave as he will, he may take kindness and relaxation as far as he possibly can, the time will come when he will have to repeat with his own hands the act of murder previously perpetrated against the patient. In contrast to the original murder, however, he is not allowed to deny his guilt.
>
> (p. 52)

How exhausting this war of the worlds can be—so much pain, often for the therapist as well as the patient. I was trying to think about an extreme illustration of the great struggle. I once worked with a woman who was the victim during her childhood of a long series of atrocious sexual attacks by her older brother and her cousin. The attacks took place between the ages of 4 and 10. All memory of these events vanished from her recall during her teen years and early twenties, but began to return in the early stages of her therapy. She wrote letters to me, penned in her own blood, that spoke of her hatred for herself and of the inevitability and necessity of her death. The only way I could find to forestall her suicide was to talk to her every day for a number of years. At the outset of this difficult journey, my patient was in a continuous darkness of reliving. It seemed that the only thing keeping her alive was my making myself extensively available on a daily basis. I remember being advised by several colleagues not to give her so much time, the danger being that I would be cultivating a dependency that was supposedly unhealthy. I was unable to accept this advice, and distanced myself from the persons giving it. I wondered if they were right, however, and suffered agonies of self-doubt in consequence of their warnings.

There is an opinion among many clinicians today that short-cuts in the psychotherapy of trauma are available, special procedures one can apply that circumvent the arduous struggles with overpowering flashbacks, terrifying nightmares, extended suicidal depressions, dangerous re-enactments of the traumatic histories. I am not a believer in any such methods. It seems to me much better that we take our time, if there is to be any chance of lasting therapeutic benefit.

But it is demoralizing to hear all the chatter about the latest quick fixes, when one is mired in the ordeals of the long haul. I try to tell myself that serious people do not take such talk seriously.

One may ask what happened in the therapy of the patient who was the childhood victim of sadistic sexual attacks. I will tell you. Mount Everest was taken down—with a spoon.

That is what the psychotherapy of such profound abuse feels like—leveling a 29,000-foot mountain one tiny spoonful at a time. It required a quarter century to be completed, a war of the worlds between the darkness and the light. During that long journey there were dangerous suicide attempts, physical assaults when the patient confused me with the perpetrators, distressing attempts at sexual seduction, and a remembering and reliving of each and every one of the traumatic incidents that felt like it would never end. In cases like this, the patient's experience is one of enduring something impossible to survive—he or she will say the pain is infinite and eternal. It is not. The problem is that the emotional injuries are severe and take a long time to process. That is all.

Not all our psychotherapeutic endeavors are as difficult as this one. But helping a person in whose life something has gone seriously amiss will always, as Brandchaft said, involve a struggle that is *mano a mano*, and it will be bloody. When that struggle is successful, it will also be a joy to behold.

Part 3

Is it really true that psychotherapy, if it is to be successful, must always involve the shedding of blood? Are there not examples in which therapist and patient get along well and a therapeutic process can occur without major disruption and struggle? Is it not possible that a bond of understanding can sometimes form, right from the beginning, and then a journey of overcoming serious trauma occurs in a context of sustaining trust and cooperation? Is every case in which patient and therapist remain in harmony to be seen as some sort of compliant surrender to authority, as in the account of the analysis given in Part 1 of this essay? Here are my thoughts on these questions.

It has been my experience that there is always blood—but sometimes the bleeding does not occur in a clashing inside the psychotherapeutic relationship. For example, I worked for 35 years with a woman who saw me as entirely benign throughout the journey; there was never any tension between us, our interchanges were always friendly, and she often told me I was a "miracle" in her life and her "sheltering port in the storm." Very significant therapeutic change occurred in the long course of our relationship. She had, as a child, been the victim of the worst sexual abuse I have encountered in a half-century of clinical practice. Her father had used her sexually once or twice each week beginning when she was two years old and extending well into her teens. The abuse was kept hidden throughout this period but was finally revealed when a visiting relative walked in on the father as he was anally raping my patient's younger brother. The family disintegrated at this point and the father was arrested. My patient, somewhat later, underwent a series of psychotic episodes that disrupted her life for the next several years. Our work then began.

I asked her to tell me about her childhood experiences in our first meeting. She gave an account of the father's sexual assaults, which had taken place in her bedroom in the middle of the night and in her bathroom when he and she were alone in the house. Describing the bathroom incidents in particular, which included oral, vaginal, and anal penetrations, she began to tremble and told me of recurring images that had appeared in her dreams during the period of her hospitalizations. The dreams were about brown paper bags delivered to her home, filled with raw, bleeding meat. The bags were oozing blood and beginning to fall apart on her living room floor. She was unable to say anything about these horrifying images, but it seemed apparent that the disintegrating bags symbolized the breakdown of the dissociation that she had used to deal with her abuse history, and she was being flooded by terrible memories and feelings. As I listened to her story, I felt I was being drenched by the blood from the raw meat. It was an awful sensation, making me want to throw up. A picture came into my mind that my patient had been slaughtered.

She and I got along exceptionally well for the next three decades and more, and there was never even the slightest friction between us. But our work began in a blood bath. The psychotherapy of individuals in whose lives something has gone seriously wrong is always a challenging struggle, but the battle does not always take the form of conflict between patient and therapist. Sometimes, as in this case, there is an understanding that is established from the outset, a lasting emotional alliance that provides a bridge to a world beyond the injuries of the past. The work, however, at some point always becomes very hard, and any attempt to circumvent the difficulty will make things worse rather than better.

My examples thus far have involved blood, literal and metaphorical, but the arduous journey of psychotherapy shows itself with many faces. Sometimes there is a long-lasting war between the darkness and the light; or a painful ascent up a high mountain involving endless reverses; or the construction of a castle, stone by stone, that keeps falling down until finally it stands securely in place. Often, though, the blood appears.

I once met a woman, early in my career as a teacher, who told me she wanted to interview me about my interest in parapsychology. As I unsuspectingly answered a series of her questions about my studies of telepathy and other paranormal phenomena, she reached into her purse and pulled out a glass and a small hammer. She struck the glass, shattering it, and began to slice her wrist and bleed on to the floor of my office. I jumped on her to stop her cutting and wrapped her wrist in a towel to arrest the bleeding. It was apparent that we were at the beginning of a long journey into darkness. The many traumas that came to the surface in the ensuing years centered on emotionally catastrophic medical interventions, including repeated major surgeries that had taken place in her early and middle childhood years. This all occurred in a context of a family that otherwise treated her with abuse and neglect. I eventually came to understand that by cutting herself before my eyes and bleeding on my floor she was opening a doorway into an early surgery-world she had experienced as cruelly persecutory.

It is good that the blood flows. How else can the truth be found and told? If there is no blood, it is unlikely that much of real value has happened (Atwood, 2017).

Dialogue

RDS: You have presented some characteristically evocative and persuasive clinical examples, George. But when you claim, "There *must be* blood," or "There is *always* blood," are you not positing a universal? Is this the form your own "metaphysical impulse" is taking?

GEA: This little chapter was written in a kind of trance, composed in my mind as I walked in the water along the shore by my summer home in beautiful Rangeley, Maine. I know that the image of blood has a special personal meaning for me—a colleague, noting how often I use the word, once suggested I have a crucifixion complex, unconsciously seeing myself as shedding blood for the world. Be that as it may, I would not want to be nailed to the Cross of an overly literal reading of my title, "There must be blood." What I am trying to say is that psychoanalytic therapy, if it is to be successful in any way, includes a resurrection within the analytic relationship of the patient's trauma history, a reliving of ancient injuries and struggles that is always painful, metaphorically—and all too often quite literally—bloody. I don't think of this as a metaphysicalizing universalization.

RDS: How does this relate to the two types of therapists you have formulated?

GEA: This question raises the issue of the blood shed by the analyst in the process of psychotherapy. Inasmuch as the trajectory of the analyst's life has been one of filling in for a lost or emotionally unavailable parent, he or she will be returned to personal traumatic scenes when the going gets rough in the course of the therapy. As you know, Bob, I classify myself as a "Type 2 Clinician," one in whom the theme of caregiving is largely based in an identification with a beloved parent who has been lost. When my patient's history of abandonment and betrayal comes alive in our relationship, and I find myself being experienced as deserting and otherwise inflicting great harm, my own childhood history of devastation in the wake of my mother's death opens up again. I sometimes have felt crucified by patients' accusations, which can be like nails driven into my flesh, and the bleeding can be severe. If I fall off the tightrope of emotional dwelling on the side of becoming swept into my patient's reality, I begin to feel like a destroyer, someone committing unforgivable crimes against humanity. The pull is strong then to recoil from such violence and leap off the tightrope on the side of affirming my own personal reality, stopping the bleeding but at my patient's expense. What I generally try to do, with very uneven success, is stay on the rope, emotionally dwelling as best I can with my patient's experience, acknowledging what I have done and not done that lends itself so profoundly to how I am being perceived, but simultaneously trying to hold on to a positive vision of what my goals and purposes are. I sometimes tell myself I must bear with the crucifixion, endure it, avoid bleeding to death in the process, in the hope that eventually the darkness that has invaded the psychotherapeutic bond will recede and I can climb down from the Cross. I guess I do have quite a crucifixion complex.

RDS: Does your so-called complex include an element corresponding to the Resurrection?

GEA: Yes. It is as if I am nailed to the Cross and die a thousand deaths—but when the therapy is successful, and the patient's trauma history quiets down and becomes more integrated, my enduring identification with my mother is restored, none the worse for wear. Jesus Christ rises from the dead.

RDS: You have described what can happen in psychotherapy for the Type 2 Clinician, one whose career choice has been influenced by an identification with a lost parent. How about your so-called Type 1 Clinician, the therapist whose work is rooted in a background of empathic caregiving to a depressed or otherwise emotionally disturbed parent? What are the special challenges such a therapist may encounter when the patient's traumas begin to surface and become relived within the psychotherapeutic dialogue?

GEA: The dream of the Type 1 Clinician, drawing on his "training" as a psychotherapist from an early age, is to give an enveloping experience of so much empathy, such a perfect attuning, that the patient will heal and thrive on the basis of this provision alone. Often, in the first stages of the therapy, a merger-like bliss can appear, one wherein the patient feels understood and supported as never before. The agony here commences when, inevitably, the analyst's efforts fail, and the patient's traumas then begin to rematerialize in their relationship. The clinician, whose personal world and professional identity are organized around soothing responsiveness, will now find himself or herself to be the cause of the patient's distress, turning his dream into a nightmare, and so the bleeding begins. What is required of the analyst here is a staying with the patient's suffering and a validating acknowledgement of what the analyst has done that contributes to a retraumatizing experience in the therapeutic dialogue. If there is a fall off the tightrope of emotional dwelling into the patient's reality, the disaster will be felt as all-consuming and the therapist's pain can become unendurable. If the fall takes place instead on the side of maintaining the clinician's reality, the patient will be pathologized and blamed for the disruptions, potentially repeating his or her trauma history in full. In the actual conduct of psychotherapy of patients whose lives include significant emotional injury, there will always be falls on the one side or the other, and there will therefore always be blood.

RDS: In striking contrast with traditional injunctions to approach each patient as a neutral blank screen or empty container, to the "exclusion of memory and desire" (Bion, 1967, p. 281), George, you have shown dramatically that the comportment of emotional dwelling entails *full-blooded* participatory engagement with patients' suffering.

12
CONCLUDING DIALOGUE

RDS: Throughout our nearly half-century-long collaboration, the one thing that has united us is our steadfast dedication to phenomenological inquiry. The power of phenomenology has shown itself in the work with extreme states, in the understanding and therapeutic approach to trauma, in the formulation of a therapeutic comportment (dwelling), in the deconstruction of metaphysical and ideological illusion, etc., etc.

GEA: This shared commitment has also united us in opposition to Cartesian trends in contemporary psychoanalysis and psychiatry, and I think accounts for the resistance we have encountered in pursuing our phenomenological dream.

RDS: We began systematizing our phenomenological method in our early studies of the subjective origins of psychoanalytic theories (Stolorow and Atwood, 1979). In each case (Freud, Jung, Reich, and Rank), we were able to articulate the central themes in the author's life along with the thematic pattern governing the author's theory, and we found striking connections between the two. Over the subsequent 40 years, this phenomenological method was further refined and extended to a range of phenomena, including the lives and works of post-Cartesian philosophers, ourselves included.

GEA: I had a sense, Bob, that following the tragedy of your late wife's death in 1991, applying phenomenological inquiry to your own emotional experience provided a pathway to the existential significance of emotional trauma.

RDS: Yes, I relived that experience at a conference in 1992—what I call a *portkey* to trauma—and wrote a little article years later (Stolorow, 1999) describing the phenomenology of my traumatized state. Two years after that, I was doing a careful reading of Heidegger's (1927) *Being and Time* and was blown away when I came upon his description of the phenomenology of existential anxiety. Both Heidegger's phenomenology of *Angst* and my phenomenology of trauma contained the same two essential elements: a painful sense of isolation and estrangement from others and a loss of the significance of the everyday world. In Heidegger's account, *Angst* comes about when one must confront death as one's "ownmost" possibility. So, trauma, I concluded, plunges one into a form of what Heidegger calls "authentic Being-toward-death." In trauma, one comes face-to-face with one's own finitude and the finitude of all those one loves.

GEA: I think I know what your answer will be, but please explain how elucidating the phenomenology of trauma helped you in formulating a therapeutic comportment to it.

RDS: Yes, I know that you already know this, George. There is a second crucial dimension in the phenomenology of trauma; in addition to its existential significance, there is its context-embeddedness. Trauma entails an experience of unbearable emotional pain, and painful affect becomes unbearable when it cannot find a context of emotional understanding—a "relational home"—in which it can be held. Painful feelings that have to be experienced alone become unendurable. It follows that the proper therapeutic comportment to emotional trauma is what I—and we—call *emotional dwelling*. Eschewing any effort to reassure, one leans into the emotional pain, saying the unsayable, articulating the unendurable, so that it can find a home in which it can be held, better borne, and eventually integrated.

GEA: I remember a walk along the ocean In Los Angeles that took place in 1991, less than two weeks after the death of your beloved wife Dede. You were telling me you felt numb and mentally paralyzed, and you offered the following interpretation of this experience: "I think it is trauma." It seemed that you were beginning to take in the magnitude of the devastating shock you had endured in awakening only a few days earlier to find that Dede had died. I listened to you as you spoke of the violence of that shock, and I wept. I trace the turn in your intellectual interests toward the phenomenology of trauma to this moment, in the immediate aftermath of the greatest loss you had experienced in your life up to that point in time. I recall our walk as if it were yesterday—it took place around five o'clock in the afternoon, under a cloudy sky. I was doing my best to be a brother and provide a space in which you could speak of the unbearable tragedy.

RDS: In the ensuing months and years, George, you were the one who related most closely to what I was going through. Unlike so many others who tried to reassure me and express hope for my future, you stayed with the devastation, validating the impossibly difficult pain I continued to feel. You said things like, "You are a destroyed man," and, "Bob, you are riding on a train to nowhere," mirroring exactly what I was experiencing. The encouraging messages I received from so many others left me feeling alone and alienated, like an alien being.

GEA: And now you have suffered a second catastrophic loss, Bob: the sudden death of your beloved daughter Emily, on her twentieth birthday. This new tragedy, itself occurring in the ongoing context of your very serious, life-threatening illness, registered with me in apocalyptic terms. I had a dream on the first night after you called to tell me that Emily had died; the dream was that I was living in a big house, and the whole back half of that house had been blown up and obliterated by a nuclear explosion. It was a terrible nightmare. That house, now half gone, was you and your world, shattered once again. My dream was an empathic identification with your experience, a putting of myself in your place and a vivid experiencing of the overwhelming loss. I was emotionally dwelling with you through my dream, leaning into your newly destroyed family.

RDS: You continue to be my brother-in-darkness, George, and now I get to be yours too, as you face the devastating illness from which your wife Liz is suffering. We are quite the pair.

GEA: Quite the pair indeed—two old men, broken by sickness, broken-hearted again and again by tragic losses, turning to each other in our shared intellectual projects and in our lasting friendship.

Speaking of projects, understanding the existential significance of trauma has had broadening implications for our critique of psychoanalytic metapsychologies, which began with our psychobiographical studies of psychoanalytic theories.

RDS: Yes, and here we are indebted to Wilhelm Dilthey's precocious phenomenological insights into what he called the *metaphysical impulse* as an evasion of human finitude. Metaphysics, of which metapsychologies are a species, postulates universal truths and everlasting grounding entities as antidotes to the limitedness and transience of human existence. We have found support for Dilthey's thesis in the *phenomenology of language*, specifically in Wittgenstein's account of how the meanings of words are created through the projection of pictures, which then become illusory metaphysical entities.

GEA: And this phenomenological understanding holds important implications for grasping the genesis of destructive ideologies, right?

RDS: Absolutely (if you'll excuse the expression)! Totalitarian ideologies can be shown to have metaphysical entities, such as "forces" of good and evil, at their core. The positing of such entities is a way of evading the existential vulnerabilities exposed by collective trauma. Emotional dwelling is invaluable as a therapeutic approach to both individual and collective trauma, holding enormous importance in our current socio-political circumstances.

GEA: How can "emotional dwelling," an activity occurring in the psychotherapeutic process, be applied to collective trauma and its aftermath? I suppose part of the answer would be that in setting national policy we recognize the impact of our shared experience of trauma—such as in 9/11—that drives us toward a Manichean binary solution pitting good against evil. Equally important would be that we perceive the captivity of our adversaries to *their* traumatic histories and associated metaphysicalizing reactions.

RDS: Yes. Imagine a world of far greater solidarity and mutual understanding than exists now—one in which there is a shared awareness and acceptance of the inescapable finitude of human existence, a world in which we can relate to one another as "siblings in the same darkness" (Stolorow, 2011). In such an enlightened world, metaphysical groundings recede and the Manichean impulse can accordingly be resisted.

⋆ ⋆ ⋆

RDS: In retrospect, I regret that we named our perspective *intersubjective-systems theory*, an appellation that has really caught on. Our original name, *psychoanalytic phenomenology*, better captures our assiduous devotion to phenomenological inquiry—a devotion grounding all of our important discoveries and formulations, including the context-embeddedness of all aspects of emotional experience and disturbance. Perhaps *phenomenological contextualism* captures it all.

GEA: Why do we need to give our perspective a name? Do we have to describe our ideas as an "ism"? Please, no more "isms." I think of our work as a set of proposals and possibilities rather than as any kind of coherent system or defined school of thought. It is a partial scaffolding at most, an incomplete structure to be developed further by those following in our phenomenological footsteps. Our life work is kind of like the bounty hunter played by Clint Eastwood in Sergio Leone's spaghetti western trilogy—"the man with no name." We are the nameless bounty hunters of contemporary psychoanalysis, wandering toward an uncertain future. I propose we leave it at that.

RDS: Well said, George. "Isms" convey a dedication to metaphysical absolutes, and the name *intersubjective system* can readily morph into a metaphysical entity as described by Wittgenstein. From now on, no more "isms"!

REFERENCES

American Psychiatric Association (2013). *Diagnostic and Statistical Manual of Mental Disorders, 5th Edition*. Arlington, VA: American Psychiatric Publishing.

Arendt, H. (1951). *Totalitarianism*. New York: Harcourt.

Aron, L. (1996). *A Meeting of Minds*. Hillsdale, NJ: The Analytic Press.

Atwood, G.E. (1978). On the origins and dynamics of messianic salvation fantasies. *International Review of Psycho-Analysis*, 5, 85–96.

Atwood, G.E. (1983). The pursuit of being in the life and thought of Jean-Paul Sartre. *Psychoanalytic Review*, 70, 143–162.

Atwood, G.E. (2011). *The Abyss of Madness*. New York: Routledge.

Atwood, G.E. (2017). The bloody amputation: A first dream in an analysis. *American Journal of Psychoanalysis*, 77, 78–82.

Atwood, G.E., Orange, D.M., and Stolorow, R.D. (2002). Shattered worlds/psychotic states. *Psychoanalytic Psychology*, 19 (2), 281–306.

Atwood, G.E. and Stolorow, R.D. (1984). *Structures of Subjectivity: Explorations in Psychoanalytic Phenomenology*. Hillsdale, NJ: The Analytic Press.

Atwood, G.E. and Stolorow, R.D. (2012). The demons of phenomenological contextualism: A conversation. *Psychoanalytic Review*, 99, 267–286.

Atwood, G.E. and Stolorow, R.D. (2014). *Structures of Subjectivity: Explorations in Psychoanalytic Phenomenology and Contextualism, 2nd Edition*. New York: Routledge.

Atwood, G.E., Stolorow, R.D., and Orange, D.M. (2011). The madness and genius of post-Cartesian philosophy: A distant mirror. *Psychoanalytic Review*, 98, 263–285.

Binswanger, L. (1946). The existential analysis school of thought, trans. E. Angel. In *Existence: A New Dimension in Psychiatry and Psychology*, ed. R. May, E. Angel, and H. Ellenberger. New York: Basic Books, 1958, pp. 191–213.

Binswanger, L. (1963). *Being-in-the-World*. New York: Basic Books.

Bion, W.R. (1967). Notes on memory and desire. *Psychoanalytic Forum*, 2, 279–281.

Bleuler, E. (1911). *Dementia Praecox of the Group of Schizophrenias*. Madison, CT: International Universities Press. 1950.

Boss, M. (1963). *Psychoanalysis and Daseinsanalysis*, trans. L. Lefebre. New York: Basic Books.

Boss, M. (1979). *Existential Foundations of Psychology and Medicine.* Northvale, NJ: Jason Aronson.

Brandchaft, B., Doctors, S., and Sorter, D. (2010). *Toward an Emancipatory Psychoanalysis.* New York: Routledge.

Braver, L. (2007). *A Thing of This World: A History of Continental Anti-Realism.* Evanston, IL: Northwestern University Press.

Braver, L. (2012). *Groundless Grounds: A Study of Wittgenstein and Heidegger.* Cambridge, MA: MIT Press.

Davis, W.A. (2006). *Death's Dream Kingdom: The American Psyche Since 9/11.* Ann Arbor, MI: Pluto Press.

Descartes, R. (1641). *Meditations.* Buffalo, NY: Prometheus Books, 1989.

Des Lauriers, A.M. (1962). *The Experience of Reality in Childhood Schizophrenia.* New York: International Universities Press.

Dilthey, W. (1910). *Selected Works: Vol. 3. The Formation of the Historical World in the Human Sciences.* Princeton, NJ: Princeton University Press, 2002.

Dilthey, W. (1926). *Meaning in History*, ed. H. Rickman. London: Allen & Unwin, 1961.

Duke, P. and Hochman, G. (1992). *A Brilliant Madness.* New York: Bantam Books.

Ferenczi, S. (1932). *The Clinical Dairy of Sandor Frenczi*, ed. J. Pupont, trans. M. Balint and N. Jackson. Cambridge, MA: Harvard University Press, 1988.

Frances, A. (2013). The new crisis of confidence in psychiatric diagnosis. *Annals of Internal Medicine*, 159 (3), 221–222.

Freud, S. (1912). Recommendations to physicians practicing psychoanalysis. *Standard Edition*, 7, 109–120. London, UK: Hogarth Press, 1958.

Freud, S. (1926). Inhibitions, symptoms, and anxiety. *Standard Edition*, 20, 77–175. London, UK: Hogarth Press, 1959.

Fromm-Reichman, F. (1954). An intensive study of twelve cases of manic-depressive psychosis. In *Psychoanalysis and Psychotherapy: Selected Papers.* Chicago, IL: University of Chicago Press, pp. 227–274.

Gadamer, H.-G. (1975). *Truth and Method, 2nd Edition*, trans. J. Weinsheimer and D. Marshall. New York: Crossroads, 1991.

Golding, S.L., Atwood, G.E., and Goodman, R. (1965). Anxiety and two cognitive forms of resistance to the idea of death. *Psychological Reports*, 18 (2), 359–364.

Greenberg, J. (1964). *I Never Promised You a Rose Garden.* Orlando, FLA: Holt, Rinehart, & Winston.

Heidegger, M. (1927). *Being and Time*, trans. J. Macquarrie and E. Robinson. New York: Harper and Rowe, 1962.

Heidegger, M. (1968). Time and being. In *On Time and Being*, ed. J. Stambaugh. Chicago, IL: University of Chicago Press, 1972, pp. 1–24.

Husserl, E. (1900, 1913). *The Shorter Logical Investigations*, ed. J. Findlay, trans. D. Morgan. New York: Routledge, 2001.

Inkpin, A. (2016). *Disclosing the World: On the Phenomenology of Language.* Cambridge, MA: MIT Press.

Jamison, K. (1995). *An Unquiet Mind.* New York: Alfred A. Knopf.

Jaspers, K. (1913). *General Psychopathology.* Chicago, IL: University of Chicago Press, 1963.

Kazantzakis, N. (1955). *The Last Temptation of Christ*, trans. P. Bien. New York: Simon & Schuster, 1960.

Khan, M. (1963). The concept of cumulative trauma. In *The Privacy of the Self.* Madison, CT: International Universities Press, pp. 42–58.

Klein, G.S. (1976). *Psychoanalytic Theory: An Exploration of Essentials.* Madison, CT: International Universities Press.

Kohut, H. (1959). Introspection, empathy, and psychoanalysis: An examination of the relationship between mode of observation and theory. In *The Search For the Self*, ed. P. Ornstein. New York: International Universities Press, pp. 205–232.

Kohut, H. (1966). Forms and transformations of narcissism. *Journal of the American Psychoanalytic Association*, 14, 243–272.

Kohut, H. (1968). The psychoanalytic treatment of narcissistic personality disorders. *The Psychoanalytic Study of the Child*, 23, 86–113.

Kohut, H. (1971). *The Analysis of the Self.* Madison, CT: International Universities Press.

Kohut, H. (1977). *The Restoration of the Self.* Madison, CT: International Universities Press.

Kohut, H. (1984). *How Does Analysis Cure?*, eds. A. Goldberg and P. Stepansky. Chicago, IL: University of Chicago Press.

Laing, R.D. (1959). *The Divided Self.* London: Tavistock Publications.

Laing, R.D. (1976). *The Facts of Life*. New York: Penguin.

Lear, J. (2006). *Radical Hope: Ethics in the Face of Cultural Devastation*. Cambridge, MA: Harvard University Press.

May, R. (1950). *The Meaning of Anxiety*. New York: W.W. Norton.

May, R., Angel, E., and Ellenberger, H. (Eds) (1958). *Existence: A New Dimension in Psychiatry and Psychology*. New York: Basic Books.

Merleau-Ponty, M. (1945). *Phenomenology of Perception*, trans. Colin Smith. New York: Routledge and Kegan Paul, 1962.

Miller, A. (1982). *The Drama of the Gifted Child*. New York: Basic Books.

de Mul, J. (2004). *The Tragedy of Finitude: Dilthey's Hermeneutics of Life*. New Haven, CT: Yale University Press.

Nietzsche, F. (1882). *The Gay Science*, trans. W. Kaufmann. New York: Vintage, 1974.

Nietzsche, F. (1886). *Beyond Good and Evil*. In *Basic Writings of Nietzsche*, ed. and trans. W. Kaufmann. New York: Modern Library, 2000, pp. 179–435.

Nietzsche, F. (1887). On the genealogy of morals. In *Basic Writings of Nietzsche*, ed. and trans. W. Kaufmann. New York: Modern Library, 2000, pp. 437–599.

Nietzsche, F. (1892). *Thus Spoke Zarathustra*, trans. W. Kaufmann. New York: Penguin, 1966.

Orange, D.M., Atwood, G.E., and Stolorow, R.D. (1997). *Working Intersubjectively: Contextualism in Psychoanalytic Practice*. Hillsdale, NJ: The Analytic Press.

Peirce, C.S. (1931–1935). *Collected Papers of Charles Sanders Peirce: Vols. 1–6*, eds. C. Harteshorne and P. Weiss. Cambridge, MA: Harvard University Press.

Putnam, H. (1990). *Realism with a Human Face*. Cambridge, MA: Harvard University Press.

Ratcliffe, M. (2008). *Feelings of Being: Phenomenology, Psychiatry, and the Sense of Reality*. Oxford: Oxford University Press.

Ratcliffe, M. (2015). *Experiences of Depression: A Study in Phenomenology*. Oxford: Oxford University Press.

Ricoeur, P. (1977). Patocka, philosopher and resister. *Telos*, 31, 152–155.

Rilke, R.M. (1910). *The Notebooks of Malte Laurids Brigge*. New York: W.W. Norton, 1992.

Rowling, J.K. (2000). *Harry Potter and the Goblet of Fire*. New York: Scholastic Press.

Sartre, J.-P. (1943). *Being and Nothingness*. New York: Washington Square Press,1966.

Shapiro, D. (1965). *Neurotic Styles*. New York: Basic Books.

Socarides, D.D. and Stolorow, R.D. (1984/1985). Affects and selfobjects. *The Annual of Psychoanalysis*, 12/13, 105–119.

Stanghellini, G. and Aragona, M., eds. (2016). *An Experiential Approach to Psychopathology: What Is It Like to Suffer from Mental Disorders?* Basel: Springer.

Stolorow, R.D. (1969). Anxiety and defense from three perspectives. *Psychiatric Quarterly*, 43, 685–710.

Stolorow, R.D. (1970). Mythic consonance and dissonance in the vicissitudes of transference. *American Journal of Psychoanalysis*, 30, 178–179.

Stolorow, R.D. (1972). On the phenomenology of anger and hate. *American Journal of Psychoanalysis*, 32, 218–220.

Stolorow, R.D. (1976). Radical surgery for psychoanalysis. Book review of *Psychology versus Metapsychology*, ed. M. Gill and P. Hozman. *Contemporary Psychology*, 21, 777–778.

Stolorow, R.D. (1978). The concept of psychic structure: Its metapsychological and clinical psychoanalytic meanings. *International Review of Psycho-Analysis*, 5, 313–320.

Stolorow, R.D. (1997a). Deconstructing the myth of the neutral analyst. In Current conceptions of neutrality and abstinence, reporter G. Makari. *Journal of the American Psychoanalytic Association*, 45, 1231–1239.

Stolorow, R.D. (1997b). Dynamic, dyadic, intersubjective systems: An evolving paradigm for psychoanalysis. *Psychoanalytic Psychology*, 14, 337–346.

Stolorow, R.D. (1999). The phenomenology of trauma and the absolutisms of everyday life: A personal journey. *Psychoanalytic Psychology*, 16, 464–468.

Stolorow, R.D. (2007). *Trauma and Human Existence: Autobiographical, Psychoanalytic, and Philosophical Reflections*. New York: Routledge.

Stolorow, R.D. (2009). Identity and resurrective ideology in an age of trauma. *Psychoanalytic Psychology*, 26, 206–209.

Stolorow, R.D. (2011). *World, Affectivity, Trauma: Heidegger and Post- Cartesian Psychoanalysis*. New York: Routledge.

Stolorow, R.D. (2014). Undergoing the situation: Emotional dwelling is more than empathic understanding. *International Journal of Psychoanalytic Self Psychology*, 9, 80–83.

Stolorow, R.D. (2016). Pain is not pathology. *Existential Analysis*, 27 (1), 70–74.

Stolorow, R.D. and Atwood, G.E. (1973). Messianic projects and early object-relations. *American Journal of Psychoanalysis*, 33, 213–215.

Stolorow, R.D. and Atwood, G.E. (1979). *Faces in a Cloud: Subjectivity in Personality Theory*. Northvale, NJ: Jason Aronson.

Stolorow, R.D. and Atwood, G.E. (1992). *Contexts of Being: The Intersubjective Foundations of Psychological Life*. Hillsdale, NJ: Analytic Press.

Stolorow, R.D. and Atwood, G.E. (2013). The tragic and the metaphysical in philosophy and psychoanalysis. *Psychoanalytic Review*, 100, 405–421,

Stolorow, R.D., Atwood, G.E., and Orange, D.M. (2002). *Worlds of Experience: Interweaving Philosophical and Clinical Dimensions in Psychoanalysis*. New York: Basic Books.

Stolorow, R.D., Atwood, G.E. and Orange, D.M. (2010). Heidegger's Nazism and the hypostatization of being. *International Journal of Psychoanalytic Self Psychology*, 5, 429–450.

Stolorow, R.D., Atwood, G.E., and Ross, J.M. (1978). The representational world in psychoanalytic therapy. *International Review of Psycho-Analysis*, 5, 247–256.

Stolorow, R.D., Brandchaft, B., and Atwood, G.E. (1987). *Psychoanalytic Treatment: An Intersubjective Approach*. Hillsdale, NJ: The Analytic Press.

Strozier, C. (2001). *Heinz Kohut: The Making of a Psychoanalyst*. New York: Farrar, Straus, & Giroux.

Sullivan, H.S. (1953). *The Interpersonal Theory of Psychiatry*. New York: Norton.

Taylor, C. (2016). *The Language Animal*. Cambridge, MA and London, UK: The Belknap Press of Harvard University Press.

Thelen, E. and Smith, L. (1994). *A Dynamic Systems Approach to the Development of Cognition and Action*. Cambridge, MA: MIT Press.

Vogel, L. (1994). *The Fragile "We": Ethical Implications of Heidegger's* Being and Time. Evanston, IL: Northwestern University Press.

Wilshire, B. (2004). *Get 'Em All, Kill 'Em!: Genocide, Terrorism, Righteous Communities*. Lanham, MD: Lexington Books.

Wittgenstein, L. (1953). *Philosophical Investigations*. Malden, MA: Blackwell Publishing.

Zahavi, D. (2005). *Subjectivity and Selfhood: Investigating the First-Person Perspective*. Cambridge, MA: MIT Press.

INDEX

absolutisms 16, 61–62
affectivity, emotional trauma 59–63
Aiken, Henry 7
anxiety, existential 74–76, 108, 128
Arendt, Hannah 97, 101
Aron, Lewis 58
Atwood, George: dialogue regarding emotional dwelling 124–126; dialogue regarding finitude of knowing 108–111; dialogue regarding Holy Ghost case 32–35; dialogue regarding intersubjective-systems theory 63–69; dialogue regarding metaphysical realm 101–103; dialogue regarding phenomenological psychopathology 77–82; dialogue regarding phenomenology 127–130; dialogue regarding selfhood 94–96; emotional dwelling 117–118, 119–124; patient who thought she was the Holy Ghost 21–32; personality and working relationship 68–69; phenomenological circle 17; philosophy 1–6, 12–14; psychiatric disorders 5; reflection and context 17–18; Stolorow, collaborations 10–12, 67–69; Stolorow, meeting 7–9
authenticity 75, 76

being-for-itself 95
being-in-itself 95
being-in-the-world 72–73
being of entities 98–99
Binswanger, Ludwig 3, 6, 11, 65
bipolar disorder *see* manic-depressive illness
Bleuler, Eugen 47–49
bloodshed, price of emotional dwelling 119–126
Boss, Medard 11, 65
Brandchaft, Bernard 49–50, 120
Braver, L. 101, 105

Cartesian perspectives: dialogue regarding phenomenology 127–130; emotional dwelling 116; intersubjective-systems theory 57–58, 65; phenomenological contextualism 16–17; psychoanalysis 13
catatonia 45–46
Catholicism, patient who thought she was the Holy Ghost 22
character: emotional dwelling 113–114; phenomenological perspective 80–81
childhood: developmental trauma 59–60, 81–82; lost childhood trauma 52–55; patient who thought she was the Holy Ghost 25–26, 33
clinical psychoanalysis 9–10, 92
clinical psychology: Atwood, George 3–5; dialogue regarding Holy Ghost case 32–35; patient who thought she was the Holy Ghost 21–32, 39–40; Stolorow, Robert 7; *see also* psychotherapy

clinical theory: psychoanalysis 92; Stolorow, Robert 9–10
coherence 88
collective trauma 99–100
constitutive context 109–110
context *see* phenomenological contextualism
Continental phenomenology 14
continuity 88
creativity, and madness 12–13, 51–52
Credos, dialogue regarding 63, 68–69, *for Atwood see* psychological disturbances; psychotherapy, *for Stolorow see* intersubjective–systems theory

Dasein 73
Davis, W. A. 100
delusions 15–16, 22, 27, 31, 34
dementia praecox 48
Descartes, René 57–58, 72–73
Des Lauriers, Austin: Atwood, George 3–4, 5; dialogue regarding Holy Ghost case 32–35; patient who thought she was the Holy Ghost 21–32; psychoanalytic phenomenology 21
destructive ideologies 129
developmental dimension 107
developmental trauma 59–63, 81–82
Dewey, John 1
diagnosis: illusion of perceptible essences 86; madness 38–39; manic-depressive illness 49–50, 79–80; phenomenological psychopathology 72–74, 78–79; schizophrenia 47–49, 78–79
Diagnostic and Statistical Manual of Mental Disorders (DSM) 72–74, 86
Dilthey, Wilhelm 40, 87–88, 91–92, 129
dimensionalization 8
dissociation 75, 123
drive, emotional trauma 59–63
Duke, Patty 44

early experiences *see* childhood
Einstein, Albert 6
emotional dwelling 62–63, 113, 117–118; becoming the patient 115–116; empathic immersion 116–117; evenly hovering attention 114; objectification 113–114; participant observation 114–115; price of 119–126; traumatization 121–123, 128–130
emotional trauma: and existential anxiety 74–76; intersubjective-systems theory 59–63; phenomenology 127–130; siblings in the same darkness 100–101; therapeutic implications 76–77
emotions, illusion of spatial location 86
empathic immersion 116–117
evenly hovering attention 114
everyday life, illusion in 88
evil, phenomenology of 101–102
existential anxiety 74–76, 77, 108, 128
existentialism 3
existential structures 11, 65, 73, 77
experiential selfhood 86

Ferenczi, Sandor 115–116
finitude 87–89, 91–92, 93, 95
finitude of knowing 105–111
Freud, Sigmund: emotional trauma 59, 60–61; evenly hovering attention 114; intersubjective-systems theory 57–58; psychoanalysis 2–3, 42; traumatization 54
Fromm-Reichman, Frieda 50

Gadamer, H.-G.: hermeneutical philosophy 15; prejudice 106, 116–117; traumatization 16
Grace (patient): dialogue regarding clinical case 32–35; patient who thought she was the Holy Ghost 21–32; secrets of the mind 39–40

Harry Potter analogy 75–76
Heidegger, Martin: Atwood and Stolorow 10; Atwood, George 3; emotional trauma 62; existential anxiety 74, 75; existential structures 11, 65, 73, 77; finitude 88, 91–92; finitude of knowing 106; metaphysical realm 98–99; phenomenological contextualism 16–17; psychoanalysis 11; Stolorow, Robert 6
hermeneutical philosophy: Dasein 73; Stolorow, Robert 15

hermeneutic attitude 106
humanism, future of 45
Husserl, Edmund 10

illusion: in everyday life 85–86, 88; metaphysics 85–89, 91–92, 109–110; perceptible essences 73, 86; spatial location 86; transparency 86–87
Inkpin, Andrew 85
inpatient service, psychiatric disorders 4–6
intelligence, and metaphysical language 94
intersubjective field 59, 61, 67, 107, 110–111
intersubjective-systems theory 57–58; developmental trauma 82; dialogue 63–69; emotional trauma 59–63; intersubjectivity 58–59; objectification 114; phenomenological contextualism 57, 58, 63–64, 106–107; as term 130
'isms' 130

James, William 1
Jaspers, Karl 71
joy, psychotherapy 42–44
Jung, Carl 2–3, 41, 54

Klein, George S. 9–10, 92
knowing, finitude of 105–111
Kohut, Heinz: emotional dwelling 116, 117; narcissistic disorders 7; the self 92–93

Laing, R. D. 65
language: dialogue regarding terms 130; and intelligence 94, 97; nature of 96; phenomenology of 85–89; the self 93, 94
lost childhood trauma 52–55

madness: and creativity 12–13, 51–52; joy and suffering 43; psychological disturbances 37–39, 40; psychotherapy 51–52
manic-depressive illness: diagnosis 49–50, 79–80; psychological disturbances 42, 44; psychotherapy 49–50
May, Rollo: Atwood, George 3; Stolorow, Robert 6
mental diseases, and psychological disturbances 39, 41–42
metaphysical dualism 72–73
metaphysical impulse: illusion 91–92; emotional dwelling 124 everyday life 94–95, 97, 102–103; human finitude 87–88, 91, 95, 129; neuroscience 67; the tragic 87–88; metapsychology 94–95, 102–103
metaphysical realm 97–99; collective trauma and resurrective ideology 99–101; dialogue regarding 101–103; siblings in the same darkness 100–101
metaphysics: illusion 85–89, 91–92, 109–110; metapsychology as 17, 94; of the real 85–89; selfhood 91–94; and the tragic 87–88
metapsychology: as metaphysics 17, 94; psychoanalysis 11, 17, 92; Stolorow, Robert 9–10
Miller, Alice 52–53

narcissistic disorders 7
Nazi ideology 13, 93, 99
new humanism, future of 45
Nietzsche, Friedrich: finitude of knowing 105–106, 108–109, 110; lost childhood trauma 54

objectification, emotional dwelling 113–114
objectivity, emotional dwelling 115, 116
ontological contextualism 16–17
Orange, Donna 5

pain 59–60, 81–82
participant observation 114–115
Peirce, Charles Sanders 1, 108
perceptible essences illusion 73, 86
perception, finitude of knowing 105–106, 108–109
personality psychology 8, 9
personality theory 94
phenomenological contextualism: Atwood and Stolorow 13–14, 66–67; emotional dwelling 116–117; finitude of knowing 105–111; Heidegger, Martin 16–17; intersubjective-systems theory 57, 58, 63–64, 106–107; psychoanalysis

17, 73, 77, 79; reflection and context 17–18; as term 130
phenomenological psychopathology 71–74, 77–82
phenomenology: Atwood and Stolorow 8; concluding dialogue 127–130; of evil 101–102; future of field 45–52; philosophical pleading for subjectivity 98; Stolorow, Robert 7; unconsciousness 58
phenomenology of language 85–89, 97, 109
philosophical pleading for subjectivity 98
philosophy: Atwood, George 1–6, 12–14; hermeneutical 15, 73; and psychoanalysis 11–12; Stolorow, Robert 6–7, 14–17
political ideology 97–98, 129
portkey, emotional trauma 75–76, 127–128
post-Cartesian psychoanalysis 13, 17; *see also* intersubjective-systems theory
pragmatism 1
prejudice 106, 116–117
psychiatric diagnosis *see* diagnosis
psychiatric disorders, inpatient service 4–6
psychoanalysis: Atwood and Stolorow 10–12; Atwood, George 2–3, 5, 13; Cartesian perspectives 13; existential structures 11; intersubjective-systems theory 57–58; joy and suffering 42; manic-depressive illness 50; phenomenological contextualism 17, 73, 77, 79; and philosophy 11–12; Stolorow, Robert 7; the tragic 92–93; *see also* clinical psychoanalysis
psychoanalytic delusions 15–16, 22, 27, 31, 34
psychoanalytic phenomenology 21; Atwood and Stolorow 8–9, 10–12; Atwood, George 12–13; dialogue regarding case study 32–35; patient who thought she was the Holy Ghost 21–32, 39–40; as term 130
psychological disturbances: future of field 45–52; joy and suffering 42–44; lost childhood trauma 52–55; madness 37–39, 40; secrets of the mind 39–42
psychopathology: phenomenological 71–74, 77–82; Stolorow, Robert 6
psychotherapy: emotional dwelling 113–118, 119–126; emotional trauma 76–77; future of field 45–52; joy and suffering 42–44; lost childhood trauma 52–55; madness 37–39, 51–52; manic-depressive illness 49–50; schizophrenia 47–49; secrets of the mind 39–42; *see also* clinical psychology

Ratcliffe, Matthew 71–72, 74–75, 77
the real 85–89, 92
recovery, trauma 62, 76
reflection: future of field 45; phenomenological contextualism 17–18
relational home 62–63, 67, 75–77, 100, 128
relational perspectives in psychoanalysis 65–66; *see also* emotional dwelling
religion, and humanism 45
religious experience, patient who thought she was the Holy Ghost 21–32, 39–40
repetitive dimension 107
resurrective ideology 99–101
Ricoeur, P. 97, 98, 99
Rilke, Rainer Maria 51–52
Rutgers University 7–8

Sartre, Jean-Paul 10, 95
the Satanic 101–102
schizophrenia: diagnosis 47–49, 78–79; psychoanalytic phenomenology 21, 32; psychological disturbances 46–47; psychotherapy 47–49
selfhood: dialogue regarding 94–96; experiential 86; language 93, 94; metaphysical impulse 91–94
self-world 64–65
siblings in the same darkness 100–101
solidity 88
spatial location illusion 86
Stolorow, Robert: Atwood, collaborations 10–12, 67–69; Atwood, meeting 7–9; dialogue regarding emotional dwelling 124–126; dialogue regarding finitude of knowing 108–111; dialogue regarding Holy Ghost case 32–35; dialogue regarding intersubjective-systems theory

63–69; dialogue regarding metaphysical realm 101–103; dialogue regarding phenomenological psychopathology 77–82; dialogue regarding phenomenology 127–130; dialogue regarding selfhood 94–96; Klein's work 9–10; lost childhood trauma 53–54; personality and working relationship 68–69; phenomenological circle 17; philosophy 6–7, 14–17; psychiatric disorders 5
subjectivity, emotional dwelling 115; *see also* intersubjective-systems theory
suffering, psychotherapy 42–44; *see also* emotional dwelling
Sullivan, Harry Stack 114–115

Taylor, Charles 96
temporal context *see* finitude
therapy *see* clinical psychology; psychotherapy
Tomkins, Silvan 8
totalitarianism 97–98, 129
the tragic 87–88, 92–93
transparency illusion 86–87
trauma recovery 62, 76
traumatization: collective 99–100; emotional dwelling 121–123, 128–130; intersubjective-systems theory 59–63, 64; lost childhood 52–55; phenomenological contextualism 67; phenomenology 127–130; Stolorow, Robert 14–17; *see also* emotional trauma
tunnel vision 75

unconsciousness 58

Vogel, L. 77

Wittgenstein, Ludwig: illusion of perceptible essences 73, 86; phenomenology of language 85–86, 89, 94, 96, 97, 129
world, as term 8

young age *see* childhood

Lightning Source UK Ltd.
Milton Keynes UK
UKHW021846161020
371545UK00012B/296